Astrology

The Ultimate Guide to the 12 Zodiac Signs, Numerology, and Kundalini Rising + A Comprehensive Guide to Tarot Reading

© Copyright 2019

All Rights Reserved. No part of this book may be reproduced in any form without permission in writing from the author. Reviewers may quote brief passages in reviews.

Disclaimer: No part of this publication may be reproduced or transmitted in any form or by any means, mechanical or electronic, including photocopying or recording, or by any information storage and retrieval system, or transmitted by email without permission in writing from the publisher.

While all attempts have been made to verify the information provided in this publication, neither the author nor the publisher assumes any responsibility for errors, omissions or contrary interpretations of the subject matter herein.

This book is for entertainment purposes only. The views expressed are those of the author alone and should not be taken as expert instruction or commands. The reader is responsible for his or her own actions.

Adherence to all applicable laws and regulations, including international, federal, state and local laws governing professional licensing, business practices, advertising and all other aspects of doing business in the US, Canada, UK or any other jurisdiction is the sole responsibility of the purchaser or reader.

Neither the author nor the publisher assumes any responsibility or liability whatsoever on the behalf of the purchaser or reader of these materials. Any perceived slight of any individual or organization is purely unintentional.

Contents

PART 1: ASTROLOGY 0

INTRODUCTION 1

CHAPTER 1: HOROSCOPES AND THEIR RISING POPULARITY 5

CHAPTER 2: THE 12 ASTROLOGICAL SIGNS AND THEIR DEEPER MEANINGS 8

CHAPTER 3: THE BIRTH CHART – WHAT IS IT AND HOW DO I READ IT? 22

CHAPTER 4: THE ASCENDANT AND HOW IT AFFECTS OUR DAILY ACTIONS AND CHOICES 33

CHAPTER 5: TAROT READING – A BRIEF HISTORY OF THE ART 39

CHAPTER 6: TAROT CARDS – THE DIFFERENT CARDS AND THEIR COMMONLY USED MEANINGS 40

CHAPTER 7: TAROT, THE STAR SIGNS AND HOW THEY WORK TOGETHER 57

CHAPTER 8: NUMEROLOGY – WHAT IS IT AND WHERE DOES IT COME FROM? 61

CHAPTER 9: YOUR NUMEROLOGY – HOW TO CALCULATE IT AND WHAT IT MEANS 65

CHAPTER 10: KUNDALINI RISING – WHAT IS IT? 93

CHAPTER 11: KUNDALINI RISING AND YOU 96

CONCLUSION 100

PART 2: TAROT 103

INTRODUCTION 104

CHAPTER 1: TAROT HISTORY 106

CHAPTER 2: THE ART OF TAROT 111

CHAPTER 3: THE CARDS 119

CHAPTER 4: THE SPREADS 162

CHAPTER 5: EXERCISES & BRAIN BOOSTERS 177

CHAPTER 6: EXTENSIONS OF TAROT 188

CONCLUSION 209

Part 1: Astrology

What You Need to Know About the 12 Zodiac Signs, Tarot Reading, Numerology, and Kundalini Rising

Introduction

Zodiac, Astrology, and other practices of divinity are everywhere – but just how much are these horoscopes truly connected to the original practices? Historically, these practices of Divinity helped people make decisions regarding agriculture, love, and war strategies. In modern day, horoscopes and the like are primarily treated like fortune cookies – fun, cute, but mostly unappreciated. The truth of the matter is that these practices have deep roots within our history as a society. In addition to this history, they also have much more complicated values and beliefs than just the surface level we see in the media. To give you, the reader, some background, here is a quick, comprehensive history of each branch of divinity covered in this book.

Since the beginning of human thought and consciousness, one part of the human existence has connected all of life. It is a part of everyday life that all humans have experienced – past, present, and future. It has brought about wonder and amazement upon all generations and all cultures and people. This is, of course, the sky. The night sky has been the subject of many a love song, or an incredible story, and is generally a magical experience. The sky above us has been used for centuries as a scientific tool, a navigational map, and (possibly the most important) a source of emotional and spiritual thought. It is due to this incredible phenomenon that we call a "sky" that we now have modern-day Astrology. However, how did we get here? To fully understand this, we have to start at the beginning – the beginning of Astrology as a thought process, that is.

The earliest observations of the night sky began with ancient Mesopotamia. The early civilizations of Mesopotamia saw the first names of our most prominent constellations and the five wandering stars. When added with the sun and the moon, these form the seven original planets. It is within this early civilization that we find the early Babylonians beginning the very science known as Astronomy (not to be confused with Astrology). It is through the studies of these ancient people that the very first studies of the "Zodiac" are produced. The Zodiac originally was a map-like distinction of the night sky – breaking up the different constellations to help judge the time of the year based on the location of certain "Wandering" stars within each constellation. Not only was this very useful from a scientific standpoint, but the different portions of the sky were also connected to different gods; thus, giving them different personality traits. This is the origin of the 12 Zodiac signs as we know them today.

The origin of modern-day Tarot cards goes back much farther than the average person may realize. The actual origin of these mystical decks is widely debated among historians, but one of the most common beliefs is that they first appeared in the 14th century in Turkey. At this time, they were most likely known as Mamluk game cards but later received their modern name from an Italian game known as "Tarrochi Appropriati", which later shortened to the modern term "Tarot".

The history of Numerology is long and widespread – almost every civilization with a hand in the formulation of mathematics connects some form of meaning to numbers. Within this book, we will focus on the three most common forms of numerology: Kabbalic, Chaldean, and Pythagorean. Kabbalic numerology originates from Hebrew mysticism with a connection to the original Hebrew alphabet. This form of Numerology is usually used to interpret names. The original Hebrew alphabet, having 22 letters, gives more significance to the Tarot deck of 22 trump cards. Chaldean Numerology is more closely related to Astrology due to its origin in ancient Mesopotamia, which we know is the ultimate origin of modern-day Astrology. Within Chaldean Numerology, each number is believed to have its own vibration and is given a level of energy from one to eight based on its energy. The final and most commonly used system of Numerology is the Pythagorean numerology, which was developed by the Greek mathematician Pythagoras. In this system of Numerology, numbers are given to the letters in the Greek alphabet based on location. This system also uses a system of vibrations but, unlike the Chaldean Numerology system, the Pythagorean system uses numbers one through nine and 11 through 22.

Kundalini Rising is certainly one of the lesser-known of the four divinities we have discussed but has very powerful ideals and origins. The actual origin of the Kundalini idea is somewhat unclear in a historical context – not much is understood of who first theorized about Kundalini and how the awakening within a person may affect them. What's found, though, is the written record of several Vedic and Tantric texts that describe Kundalini. The earliest known currently is a record by a man named Adi Sankaracharya, who lived around the seventh to eighth century AD and gave his record here: "Having filled the pathway of the Nadis with the streaming shower of nectar flowing from the Lotus feet, having resumed thine own position from out of the resplendent Lunar regions and Thyself assuming the form of a serpent of three and a half coils, sleepest thou, in the hollow of Kula Kunda (Kula Kunda means the hollow of Mooladhara Sacrum bone)."

Clearly, we can see from this that the historical context of these practices alone is much more than we make them out to be. Throughout this text, you will learn in depth about the practice and meaning behind each of these forms of Divinity. Along the way, you will find information that may help you navigate your own life through the understanding of these practices. The information regarded in the practices can help you understand why you feel the way you do, why other people may act certain ways towards you, and how to respond in certain situations to yield the most positive impact for you as an individual. All of this knowledge and more will be gained through the completion of this book!

Chapter 1: Horoscopes and Their Rising Popularity

In today's world, we are surrounded by horoscopes of varying degrees of legitimacy. From your love life to how your finances are going to go for the next week, horoscopes can tell us just about anything about our lives and how they should play out within the next day to the next year. However, in all of this, what *actually* are horoscopes? How do people decide what a Pisces should invest in this year? Have they always been around, or did they just appear out of nowhere? This chapter will discuss all of this and more as we delve deep into horoscopes and how they fit in with modern-day life.

Horoscopes refer to the predictions made based on the location of the five "Wandering Stars" (Mars, Venus, Mercury, Jupiter, and Saturn) relative to the constellation that is connected to your Zodiac sign. Each planet within the "Wandering Stars" is said to be connected to a different deity. Because of this connection, each planet has different characteristics akin to that of personality traits that affect the constellation (a.k.a. the Zodiac) they are in at that time in different ways. In Greek tradition, the gods and the traits associated with each planet were:

Mars – The God of war; a Zodiac with Mars in their constellation may experience heightened confidence and self-assertion as well as more energy and impulsiveness.

Venus - The God of love; a Zodiac with Venus in their constellation may experience more intensity within their love life as well as more inclination towards the Arts.

Mercury - The God of thievery, commerce, and travel; a Zodiac with Mercury in their constellation may have an easier time with education and have better luck economically.

Jupiter - The God of the Gods; this planet is often connected with leadership – and as such, a Zodiac with Jupiter in their constellation may feel bouts of extreme luck and optimism

Saturn - The God of agriculture and the harvest; when this planet is seen in a Zodiac's constellation, it is likely they may feel heightened senses of obligation and be more inclined to follow rules

Of course, this is a very brief look at what a planet means within your constellation. To get a real estimate of what the different planets mean within different houses of your birth chart, read Chapter 3.

Now that we understand the very basic principle of horoscopes and what they are meant to convey, how did they come to be? Why are they so popular? The beginning of daily horoscopes as we know them today started in the year 1930 when a man by the name of R. H. Naylor published the first ever newspaper horoscope. The subject of his predictions was the just-born Princess Margaret whose natal chart deemed her life would be "eventful." While not quite the complicated, spiritualistic horoscope we are used to seeing nowadays, this publication did seem to spark something that has lasted through the generations – that is, a sort of fascination within us. It began in Naylor's column with predictions based on birthdays that were happening within the following week. Throughout his time in the newspaper industry, it became more apparent that his horoscopes would need to be relevant to a wider audience to stay on the up and up. This led to Naylor using the sun signs in the method that we know very well today. Switching from specific birthdates to Sun signs allowed Naylor's predictions to apply to a much larger amount of people. Since that time, horoscopes have gotten more and more complicated and vague.

But what exactly has made these horoscopes so popular? Why are people so infatuated with paragraphs of vague descriptions of things you may or may not experience or feel within the next 24 hours? The answer is simple – you only have to look at the one thing that people have never lost fascination with: themselves. Since the beginning of time, human beings have been obsessed with themselves, and it only seems to be getting worse – the more time that we as a society have to spend doing almost nothing or reflecting upon ourselves as people, the more that we become obsessed with further understanding our personalities. Horoscopes are the perfect food for this obsession because they focus excessively on the individual and because they are almost never-ending. Every single day, there's new information about each planet within each star sign, so the person addicted to learning more about themselves can continue to do so for as long as they please. The addition of social media and new technology makes this addiction even easier to acquire. With the free information at everyone's fingertips, you can find pages upon pages about your horoscope with one simple Google search. Now you might think that it is all gloom and doom and that we are all horrible narcissists who only care about themselves – but don't worry! The enjoyment of reading horoscopes doesn't make you a bad person – just curious, for the most part. Besides, as far as addictions go, there are far worse ones than just reading your horoscope.

Chapter 2: The 12 Astrological Signs and Their Deeper Meanings

Most people nowadays know the basics behind the 12 Zodiac signs. They at least know their own Zodiac sign and some of the stereotypes behind those signs. They may even know which signs are supposed to be "compatible" with them. Truthfully, there is much more that goes into a Zodiac sign than just the stereotypical traits that modern media assigns to them. In addition, a person's personality is connected to a lot more than just the sun sign, which most of these Zodiac websites focus on. Within this chapter, we will dive deep into the intricacies of each Zodiac sign based only on their sun sign – starting at the end, for once, with Pisces.

Pisces (Feb 19 – Mar 20)

The Pisces Zodiac sign is the very last sign in the cycle of 12. Ranging from February 19 to March the 20, this sign is known as a water sign, and as such is often related to mermaids or other sea creatures. This Zodiac is commonly described as being dreamy and akin to art. These things, of course, are only surface level traits for this Zodiac. You can delve deeper into this Zodiac by looking at its star constellation, which is meant to be two fish swimming in opposite directions held together by a string or rope. These two fish, and the fact that they are swimming against each other rather than with means that someone with this sign may be very contradicting and show the traits and signs of many other Zodiacs. This particular sign can be very confusing and difficult to pin down to a set of a few traits because of its location within the 12 signs. Due to it being the last sign, the Pisces constellation is known to exhibit traits of each sign. Because of this, connection to the other signs and the duality represented by the fish in the constellation means that Pisceans are often one to see every side of the story before coming to a conclusion. Nothing is particularly black or white to them; everything is more complicated and requires more thought than a simple yes or no answer. It is because of this openness of thought that Pisceans are often connected to being artisans or musically talented. Although, being a Pisces does not mean you will be good at art or music; it may simply mean that you have an appreciation for one or the other. People often like to describe Pisceans as empathetic, which in a way is true, but not for the reasons people believe. It has nothing to do with Pisces being more soft or emotional than the other signs but more with the fact that the fish are a product of their environment. Pisces are very susceptible to changes in their environment, which can translate into empathy when people are involved in that environment.

Aquarius (Jan 20 – Feb 18)

Once again with the sign Aquarius you can begin to see the deeper values within the constellation. The art of the Aquarius is often depicted as a young boy pouring out his offering of water in a sign of modest service. Aquarius is very interesting because while it is technically an air sign, it has a very close connection to water. A huge part of the Aquarius Zodiac is the idea of rebirth and cleansing. Detachment is a word commonly used to describe an Aquarius Zodiac, giving an image of a cold, uncaring human. This is, of course, only the surface level description of the Aquarius personality. The reality is much deeper and more complex. The

Aquarius Zodiac is one that sees things the way that they truly are, without bias or prejudice. This is because of the cleansing property of this sign, which gives people of this sign the ability to see through the dirt and grime of someone's surface level traits. This trait also often allows for heightened levels of intelligence and self-awareness. There is a lot of difficulty in pinning down this sun sign's traits because, in traditional Greek philosophy, the sun and Saturn (Aquarius' traditional ruler) are sworn enemies. Having Aquarius (a product of Saturn) as a sun sign, then, can cause inner turmoil within the person in question. This individual may have difficulty understanding who they are as they grow up; they may often feel as though they have many conflicting personalities. In addition to this, because of the "detriment" of the sun (the star meant to be about the individual), a person may tend to be more concerned about others than themselves. They may tend to value the needs of the group over the needs of themselves. This once again connects to an Aquarius' ability to separate reason from emotions allowing for more logical thinkers. While this is a brilliant tool for someone to utilize when faced with difficult decisions, these signs may have difficulty feeling or accepting their own emotions. They may forget when it is okay to feel emotional and maintain a detached demeanor. This can cause problems in relationships particularly in the romantic sphere.

Capricorn (Dec 22 – Jan 19)

The Capricorn is most steadily affected by its planetary ruler Saturn than any of the others within the Zodiac. The Capricorn Zodiac relationship with Saturn is very interesting as it is akin to that of a strict father with an ambitious, outgoing son. The stereotype of the Capricorn is that of hardheadedness led by blinding ambition. And while the Capricorn is often quite ambitious, there exists much more to this ambition than meets the eye. Much like the stereotypical son of a disproving father, a Capricorn traditionally aims to accomplish, an aim that stems from wanting to prove themselves more than anything. Most descriptions of the Capricorn Zodiac tend to focus on the more negative aspects of their personality. Lack of creativity and joy is often pointed out in relation to these individuals. This is mostly due to the timing of their sign; the entirety of this sign takes place in the dead of winter when the sun sign has the least power over their personality leading to a believed lack in the common traits associated with light and the sun. This is somewhat of a misconception because while the weakness of the sun is apparent, the sun sign is not everything. As we will discuss later, an individual is made up of much more than just their star sign, and due to this weakening of the sun, a Capricorn, in particular, tends to be much more dependent upon their other houses. It is because of this dependence that Capricorns are considered very mysterious; it is not because they are all brooding and quiet but because they are more complicated and malleable. To truly understand a Capricorn and "unveil the mystery" you have to look at their whole natal chart and give more weight to the other aspects of that chart. Capricorns are typically people that have more difficult childhoods than others. Not necessarily because of outside influence; a Capricorn could have had what an outsider would consider the perfect childhood and that individual could still feel a sort of inner turmoil from this childhood for their own personal reasons. Capricorns are known to thrive in adulthood and maturity, having learned valuable life lessons from their difficult childhoods. Capricorns can be described as "old souls" whose experience and life are often underestimated in the power it bestows upon them.

Sagittarius (Nov 22 – Dec 21)

Quite the turnaround from his brother the Capricorn, Sagittarius is often described as energetic and jovial. Many traits of the Sagittarius stem from its planetary ruler, Jupiter. Many common descriptions of Sagittarians like to describe them as "on a quest for knowledge", and while this certainly can be true, it's based on correlation rather than causation. The truth of the matter is that a Sagittarius likes to throw themselves wholeheartedly into everything they do, whether that be information and learning based or something else. Sagittarians likes to do things very big; they don't halfway do anything – go big or go home is their motto for life. Looking at the Archer, which represents Sagittarius, shows us their commitment. Just as the Archer cannot stop or slow down their arrow after they've released it, once a Sagittarius starts something, there's no stopping them until they've reached completion. Also, like the Archer, Sagittarians don't recognize restrictions; they are free souls. They don't appreciate anything binding or strict; they like to live by their own will or rules. Another huge trait of a Sagittarius is honesty – the arrow is one of brutal, clear honesty. Of course, there is another side to this star sign – one rarely presented but there all the same. Sagittarians despite being ruled by Jupiter can often exhibit very Mars-like qualities. You can see this reflected in their symbol, which is not only the Archer but also the Centaur. The Centaur is an interesting mythological creature that shines a very different light onto the Sagittarius sign. The Centaur is often considered in mythology as a creature of war, giving Sagittarius a more violent, bestial side than is often portrayed in mainstream media. It is due to Sagittarius' clear reasoning skills that this side does not show itself often – which is probably for the best. It is the combination of the temperance of Jupiter with the bestiality of the Centaur that allows for a well-balanced Zodiac such as this one.

Scorpio (Oct 23 – Nov 21)

The Scorpio by far receives the most negative treatment from beliefs of the Zodiac. Many descriptors of this Zodiac would have the reader believing that Scorpios are just plain darkness and evil. But, of course, it is never that simple. No Zodiac is strictly good or bad; the Zodiac is simply a series of probable traits that get twisted and altered to each individual. Scorpio is an interesting sign because it is ruled by Mars, a planet known for producing war-like qualities and traits associated with aggression. However, Scorpio is also a water sign. Water signs are more often known for traits associated with calmness and tranquility – but a tsunami can destroy a town, and a river can wear down a rock. That is to say that the planet Mars within this sign brings out some of the fiercest qualities of water. So, while the Scorpio can exert the same power and damaging qualities of a tsunami, they also keep it hidden until the last second. The same way that the building of a tsunami is nearly undetectable on a boat in the ocean, a Scorpio's anger may not be detectable as it builds but can cause rampant chaos when released. This brings up another common quality of Scorpios – undetectable energy. Scorpio individuals chose more often than not to keep their power reserved for matters of importance, but the energy is still there. This causes a sort of magnetism that others may not even notice until they are completely drawn in by a Scorpio. It is also interesting, and somewhat contradictory, to note that the Scorpio's strongest power is their patience. One would be led to believe that by having Mars as their ruling planet that these individuals would be prone to rash decision making. However, this is not the case; Scorpios are far more determined than they are rash or impulsive. This is shown in the symbolism of Scorpions in mythology; they are typically protectors or guardians of places or things. You can also think about how a scorpion hunts as an indicator of the temperament of a Scorpio. Scorpions are vicious predators but not ones that actively hunt out their prey and kill them in cold blood; scorpions wait patiently for a victim to fall into their trap. This sign also shares a trait with his sister sign the Virgo. That is, the ability to see through superficiality. The Scorpio is impassible and sees through any falsities a person may try to present to them.

Libra (Sept 23 – Oct 22)

Libra is often associated, partly because of its sign, with balance and order. While this is true, it is not necessarily for the reasons that most people believe. While its sign is, in fact, a scale in perfect balance, this well-known trait has a much deeper meaning. This trait is due to the fact that during this time of the Libra, the sun returns in its orbit to shine down upon the equator, which brings day and night back to perfect symmetry. This balance of day and night is the source of tons of symbolism of balance and equilibrium. In most ancient societies, this time was often a time of reflection on the current status of business affairs and for deciding what would be necessary for the next crop season. Libras are often considered the most "moderate" of the Zodiac. Not wanting to engage in extremes or excess, Libras often live up to this summation. The scale in Greek culture was often used as a symbol for law and judgment. To coincide with this, Libras often have exceptional gifts in analysis and impartial reasoning. Libras are often very unbiased in their opinions and decisions. One of the most important beliefs of a Libra is an innate need for fairness for all – themselves and others. Libras will do almost anything to ensure a fair decision is made for all parties involved. Libras are also very firm in their beliefs, and, while they do not care for extremes, are the first to speak up against oppressive tendencies. Despite their appearance as a desirable sign, these individuals can be a force to be reckoned with if they believe someone is being treated unfairly. These people can become incredible lawyers (which we often see in mainstream media), but they also make great teachers, police officers, and political leaders. These individuals have even been known to start revolutions. While "moderate" may be their main determinate, don't think that makes them weak or boring. In fact, this sign, when challenged, can be proven to be quite fierce. What is most interesting about Libra is that its ruling planet is Venus, a planet often described with words like "passion" or "love", which on the surface level seem to contradict Libra's previous character traits. In fact, this planet only adds a second layer to Libra's personality. This planet adds a certain need to be liked and appreciated by their peers. It also adds a level of charming grace to this individual, which is beneficial for jobs that may be good for this sign. Unfortunately, the contradictions between Venus and Libra can often lead to difficulty in relationships, especially with some of Librans' less desirable traits. Most of Libra's more difficult traits have to do with the fact that life is not inherently fair or balanced, which can lead to problems when a Libra gets too hung up on things – they cannot change to be fairer. Librans are often brilliant negotiators but can occasionally use this skill for things within their own personal interest without realizing it. This often leads to problems when someone attempts to show them their bias, as they will simply believe that the other person needs to see it through their own eyes. With determination often comes hardheadedness, unfortunately.

Virgo (Aug 23 – Sept 22)

By far, Virgo often gets the most stereotypical, almost entirely untrue, descriptions in modern media. Often described as shrewd, frigid, and shrill, Virgos are very rarely looked at in a positive light. These are, of course, only the skin-deep descriptors of Virgos; they are much more complicated and require much more research to understand fully. According to ancient societies, the gifts of the Virgo are that of grace and purity, great diplomacy and mastery of words. Known to be shy in their formative years, Virgos often underestimate their talents and skills, which leads others to believe them less skilled than they truly are. Virgos are often given traits in a negative light, such as coolness or dryness. The truth of the matter is that these are not necessarily weaknesses but strengths as well. The ability to look at life clearly without the fog of sentiment and emotion can be highly beneficial. One trait that often surprises people is that Virgos are a highly creative sign. Due to the shyness associated with this sign, this often goes unnoticed as the Virgo themselves may feel cautious about showing their creativity beyond close friends and family. It is certainly a different kind of creativity, sure, but is still brilliant and beautiful. The creative nature of the Virgo is that of near perfection. These are individuals that may produce perfectly balanced photography or be incredible interior designers, whereas other commonly known creative signs may be more drawn to messier forms of art, such as painting or sculpting. Preferring order and finding beauty in perfection and cleanliness is the Virgo's need. While a huge advantage of this sign is its affinity towards clear reason, this is often misinterpreted as being unsympathetic and insensitive. This is far from the truth, of course. Virgos are often very gentle and thoughtful of others, valuing the consideration of others over themselves. These signs have a strong innate talent to form good judgments very quickly. A common issue presented with earth signs is their unwillingness to move or be flexible, but this trait is offset with the speed of Virgo's planetary ruler Mercury. The quick movements of Mercury allow for more flexibility in the personality of a Virgo while also maintaining the strength of the earth sign. Virgos are known for having little patience for abstract ideals that lack practical use. They prefer to understand ideas that are useful for practical application. Perhaps as a good balance, Virgos also do not entertain the need for unrealistic perfection. This may sound contradictory to their creative tendencies, but the fact is that while they strive for perfection, they know the limits of themselves and others and only strive for perfection that they are well aware is within their capability. It is due to this sign being an earth sign that makes them a realist rather than an idealist. Virgos are often very hard workers and can be depended upon to produce good consistent work. The only trouble with this is that they often expect the same of others as well, who may not be able to keep up with the levels of work of the Virgo.

Leo (July 23 – August 22)

Leos are often regarded as the "Kings" of the Zodiac. With the sun as their planetary ruler, these signs reap the full advantage of the sun's gifts. The most prominent feature of this sign is its symbol, the ever-powerful lion. The lion is used as a symbol is many ancient texts of power, strength, and leadership. It is no surprise that wrestling with a lion was often considered the act of the greatest heroes in ancient mythology. This is one of the few Zodiacs whose stereotypes are closer to the truth than not, for Leos are often known to be courageous, valiant individuals. The misunderstanding here is that they must be courageous in the face of physical challenges – when in reality, this courage can show itself in a variety of more complicated ways. This courage can be exhibited by trying something new and frightening or battling some sort of inner beast, such as mental illness or disease. Despite all of this perceived power and strength, the Leo can be known as a very sensitive individual. Particularly in regard to their perceived enemies, Leos can be quick to see insults in normal language or to imagine a threat and attack. The quickness of a Leo to attack does not necessarily come from their bravery or courage but their blind ego. Leos are very in tune and aware of their feelings but have a lot of trouble understanding the feelings of others. The Leo is often known for having little self-control over their actions and could benefit from the companionship of an earth sign to give them more balance over their base urges. Leos are often bragged about extraneously in mainstream zodiac columns, but very rarely do you see the dark side of the Leo spoken of. For with all of this courage and power comes a tendency towards bullying, and coupled with the lack of understanding felt by this sign can often lead to a brutal and viciously unwarranted attack. It is this trait that promotes a common theme amongst Leos that may surprise most readers. Leos have an inclination towards more evil tendencies. While this comes as a surprise to most people familiar with the symbolism of the lion, when you combine all of these characteristics, you can often find connections to less desirable actions – like that of dictators or unfair rulers.

Cancer (June 21 – July 22)

Cancers are very interesting signs because they are the exclusive holders of the planetary ruler, the Moon. These signs are symbolized by the sea crustacean the crab. It is within this symbol that we find most of the Cancer's traits – hard shell on the outside with frightening, powerful pinchers, but moist and soft on the inside. Much like the crab, many Cancers are prone to be very difficult and hard on the outside, ready to pinch any who gets too close but are quite soft and kind on the inside. The trouble with this is how difficult it is to get to this inner personality. Reaching this inner personality is often as difficult as getting to the flesh of a real crab; it requires some breaking of the outside shell and may require some tools. Also, as with the work of breaking a crab's shell, it is not for the faint of heart, and this individual will meet many people within his or her life who are not willing to go through the work of breaking through the shell and will simply prefer to get pinched. This is okay, of course; these individuals who are not willing to break through to the kinder side of the Cancer are not deserving of it in the first place. The crab as a creature is often known to exist purely on the shores of the ocean, giving it a connection to the ebb and flow of the waves upon the shore. This often translates to moodiness within a Cancer, which is a misunderstanding, as it is believed to come out of nowhere – but there is always a reason for a wave to break a certain way that just may not always be easy to see or understand. While it may appear to an outside viewer that a Cancer is up and down for no real reason, they are simply more sensitive to the world around them and are responding to things that a less sensitive individual may not notice or appreciate. This sign is often regarded as lazy and weak but anyone who believes these statements has never been pinched by a crab.

Gemini (May 21 – June 20)

To the inexperienced viewer, a Gemini may seem two-faced or fake. While the symbol for the Gemini does literally have two faces, that descriptor is not fully accurate. The Gemini emphasizes the natural need for contradiction – that is to say, you can't have one without the other. Gemini is based on the idea that opposites are a necessity to life. You cannot have a day without light, fire without water, or sadness without joy. Gemini recognizes that rather than fighting one another, humans can benefit the most from bringing two opposites together to work on their strengths and cover each other's weaknesses, to fill the gaps that the other leaves. It is due to this appreciation of opposites that enables Geminis to be skilled at almost everything they do. From communication in which they can use both rational and irrational thought to creativity in which they are unafraid to try every type of art imaginable. The Gemini's skill in communication is particularly remarkable as their ability to see all sides of a situation gives them a special kind of advantage. It is far easier to argue against an opponent's point when you fully understand their point as well as your own. It is due to this unique ability that Geminis are often very skilled lawyers and politicians. Geminis are fascinated with learning just a little bit about everything. They are often considered the "Jack of all trades" of the Zodiac with their undying thirst to learn new things. This can cause problems because while they are interested in learning about everything, they are not necessarily interested in learning *everything* about everything. They often tend to lack the quality to their knowledge in favor of the quantity of it. The Gemini possesses a unique ability to conform their views and beliefs to better fit in with their company. Because of this, it is very easy for a Gemini to make a lot of friends, making this sign very skilled at networking and professions of business.

Taurus (April 20 – May 20)

The Taurus is one of the oldest Zodiac signs with its origin connected to celebrating the domestication of the ox, a time in human history that saw a dramatic upswing in agricultural productivity and better livelihoods. Because of this, the ox is often revered for its slow, calm nature that hides an immense strength and power. This gets translated into the holders of this sign as quiet and easy-going people that get through things with step by step determination. Rather than fighting through a challenge quickly and violently, a Taurus takes a more planned and calm approach. This allows for a sort of productivity that is powerful in its simplicity. As a student, for example, where one sign may leave an assignment until the last day and rush through it, a Taurus would begin work on an assignment weeks in advance, and while they would take a long time to finish it, they would find themselves unstressed and unbothered by the daily work. These star signs are good with routine and prefer to do a little bit of work every day rather than do it all in one night. These signs are often slow to anger, but once they have been crossed, they offer no mercy to the person in question. The best descriptor of a Taurus is often "Down to earth" which is truer than people realize. As an earth sign, these Zodiac are often very grounded in reality and do not fancy themselves with wistful passions and dreams. Much like their symbol, the bull, you cannot push a Taurus towards your view. If you wish for a Taurus to see certain things from your light, you will have to guide them there gently and kindly. Taureans do not respond to attempts at force; they are remarkably good at letting harmful actions and words slide by them, and are extremely patient people. If a Taurus is angered, they tend to go through an interesting sort of inner turmoil, for it is so rare to anger these individuals that the act of doing so often renders them confused and unable to understand their feelings. Because of this confusion, they tend not to think about their actions when in this state and may express their feelings through physical means. Banging, breaking, and generally causing chaos is how a Taurus tends to express anger, not fully understanding how to vocalize the distress they are experiencing on the inside.

Aries (March 21 – April 19)

The Aries Zodiac comes at a historically very important time of the year. The time of this Zodiac falls right at the beginning of springtime or the metaphorical "Awakening" of the earth. It is this time that animals begin to come out of hibernation and crops begin to grow. This time of the year also has strong ties to fertility and rebirth. As the time of this sign suggests (and with it being the first Zodiac), this sign is often considered to awaken the rest of the Zodiac. This time of the year was often attributed with some sort of celebration, and often the Ram became a large part of this celebration, placing Aries right at the center of this integral time of the year. As a result of the timing of this sign, the sun plays a huge part in the traits associated with this sign. A sign with the sun strong in their chart often exhibits characteristics based on the sun. Aries, for instance, put a very high value on honesty and hate deceit; they like for information to be presented to them in logical, simple terms without fillers. Aries are often described in modern media as being ambitious, and this is true, but not in the way that people are used to understanding. Aries being ambitious does not necessarily mean that they wish to gain power or rule over others (although Aries do tend to make good leaders). Aries are ambitious by saying that they cannot be stopped once they set their sights on something. It doesn't particularly matter what it is, big or small; if the Aries wants to do it, they are going to do it. Aries are also often connected deeply to their personal identity and impulses – in simpler terms: they don't do small talk. "Social Niceties" do not exist for an Aries; they much prefer to say things how they are and never sugarcoat information. An Aries also has a very strong need for freedom for themselves. They crave a lack of structure; they need to be able to make their own rules in life. The downside to this trait is it can sometimes lead to squashing the freedoms of others – not intentionally by the Aries, but as a consequence of their inability to be stopped. Aries are often defined as adventurous or fearless, and while these traits do often present themselves, it is not for the sake of being adventurous. Rather, an Aries has a constant and undying need to be stimulated by new experiences and activities. This often causes them to become adventurous without them particularly setting out in search of adventure. The Aries sign is a fire sign, and it is very easy to see why. Most Aries individuals will have a certain vivacity to them, a certain outgoing personality trait that could dim the sun.

Chapter 3: The Birth Chart – What Is It and How Do I Read It?

Nearly everyone who has shown interest in Astrology has at least heard of the birth chart. The birth chart can sometimes seem like a crazy complicated system full of math and estimations that are beyond normal civilian capabilities. This is simply not true – while some aspects of the birth chart can be a little bit difficult to map out, the very basics of it come down to each planetary alignment at the time of your birth. Within this chapter, we're going to break down the different parts of your birth chart and what those different aspects mean to you as a person living your daily life. We will also give an example of a birth chart with estimations of a completely random birth date, time, and location, as well as give real-life scenarios in which these different planets may affect a people in various situations.

The Sun

This is the part everybody is familiar with, especially if you've been reading along as Chapter 2 was all about this sign. Your sun sign is based on the constellation that the sun was in on the day of your birth. This sign is typically the most focused on because it is supposed to represent the most basic parts of your personality. This includes your ego, your inner self – and much like the sun within our solar system, all of the other planetary signs are dependent upon this sign. Some astrologers relate your horoscope to a painting of you – and within this analogy, the sun sign is the outline sketch before beginning the actual painting. It is very important; it lays down the foundation for what the painting will look like, but it is not by any means complete.

The Moon

If the Sun is the outline of your self-portrait, the Moon is the color pallet. The Moon is arguably as important as the Sun within your birth chart. The moon sign describes how you feel emotions and how you express them to other people. The moon sign covers parts of you that you don't even realize are happening, little habits you do on a day-to-day basis. The moon sign shows your most basic needs for affection, and how you feel the most loved. Because of the Moon's connection with femininity and fertility, it also predicts an individual's relationship with the women in their life. This is different from the romantic relationship shown in Venus and is more likely to interactions with mothers.

Mercury

Mercury controls our intelligent side. It predicts our rationality or lack thereof. It gives us our skills in speaking, writing, or memory. Mercury often greatly affects how we learn or take in information. The knowledge of a child's sign in Mercury is very helpful in understanding how they are doing in school and how they could be helped.

Venus

Venus shows us how we love and feel the love of others. People often find that they may act very different in romantic relationships than in normal relationships. The planet Venus is a powerful planet due to the power we as a society give to romance and love. Not only does this planet affect your love life, but it also affects how you appreciate beauty. Your tastes in art and beauty can often be traced to your sign in Venus. This planet is also known for its hand in pleasure. As a result, this planet can be connected to what you like to do for fun. Due to the feminine strength of this planet, it also predicts what an individual would consider the "perfect woman". Within a woman's chart, this is often the type of woman they wish they were or strive to be, whereas, in a man's chart, this is the type of woman they are most attracted to.

Mars

Mars is most in control of physical action. Where Venus often has a hand in the spirit of a person, Mars is more attached to the actions of that person. Mars often predicts your sex drive and tendency to lust over love. Mars is the passion behind sex, the anger before a fight, and the energy before a race. Mars is the commitment to action before it happens. These are all very extreme examples, but Mars is an extreme planet. If you've ever made a rash decision that was out of your normal process, Mars may be to blame.

Jupiter

Jupiter is often considered in Astrology to be a sign of luck and optimism. Within your life, the strength of Jupiter in your chart can predict the luck or lack thereof you will experience in your lifetime. We as people experience luck in different aspects of our life – one who is gifted in wealth might not be gifted in beauty or vice-versa. So, while Jupiter is a sign of luck depending upon the constellation, it may be lucky to you in different ways. This planet also governs our philosophical views on the world and how we feel about deeper, less practical knowledge. This planet also predicts where you might devote much of your time in your life. That is, it expresses what sort of things you hold with higher importance than others.

Saturn

Not all of the planets promote good qualities of their sign. Saturn traditionally is considered the "evil" planet. While this isn't necessarily true, it is easy to see why people may believe this. Saturn is in charge of maintaining balance within the Zodiac. This can sometimes be translated into being "evil" because Saturn often has to deny the excess of the other planets. It is this denial that leads people to identify Saturn as evil because it can be interpreted as the destruction of dreams. This is, of course, a surface-level belief – if you look deeper, you can find that Saturn is the cause of motivation of the human spirit. The struggles and difficulties that Saturn can cause in a person's life are really seeds of motivation to spur an individual towards accomplishment and completion. Tough love is a better descriptor of Saturn's ruling than evil.

Transcendental Planets

Uranus, Neptune, and Pluto are known as the "Transcendental Planets" as they are not a part of the original planets included in traditional Astrology. Traditional Astrology is only based on planets visible by the naked eye; however, this doesn't mean that these other planets are worthless. These other planets have less of an impact on an individual because of their distance to us on Earth. These planets tend to exhibit more philosophical energies than the main planets – you tend to have to look harder to see the effect they have on a person.

Uranus

Uranus promotes the energy of uniqueness about a person, as well as the affinity for sudden ideas and creative solutions.

Neptune

Neptune powers our desire for escape. Neptune often drives us to read long books of magical adventure or spend time away from the stresses of everyday life.

Pluto

Because of Pluto's slow orbit, generations often share the star sign with this planet. Because of this, this planet is often associated with the similarities of generations.

These are very basic descriptions of the impact of these planets, and there are much more moving parts to an individual's birth chart. These more specific aspects of a birth chart will be discussed as you come to understand your own birth chart through the following example.

Example of a Birth Chart

Name: Joe

Birthdate: October 8, 1962

Time: 4:00 AM EST

Location: San Jose, California

> 1) To start off your birth chart, you need to know the exact time and date of your birth as well as the location. If you do not know your time of birth, you will have trouble deciphering the ascendant of your sign.
> 2) To begin calculating your birth chart, you need to know where the constellations and planets are at what times and dates. This part is a little bit difficult for someone without extreme education in Astronomy. Hence, to find your signs for your birth chart, you may want to consult a website or professional astrologer.
> 3) Most birth charts begin with a table showing the exact locations of each planet in each sign. From left to right, you

will see a planet, sign, and coordinates. The sign to the right of the planet is the constellation that the planet is in and is thus the traits that will be expressed within that portion of your personality. The coordinates are the exact astronomical location of the planet.

Sun in Libra

The sun expresses the most basic forms of an individual's personality and how you handle your day to day life.

To read more about Libra as a star sign, click back to **Chapter 2: Libra.**

Moon in Aquarius

The Moon sign expresses the unconscious emotionalism and moods of an individual.

Aquarius as a moon sign leads to extreme abilities in observation. These individuals are very interested in the reasons behind human actions, though they may not express it outright. These people may be seen as detached or shy particularly in their childhood. While these people enjoy being around people, they often find themselves feeling "different" from those around them. When it comes to their family, these individuals find themselves rebelling in their youth, and once they begin a family of their own are extremely prideful of their children and spouses. After maturing, Lunar Aquarius' tend to find messier unpractical emotions as unnecessary and pride themselves on keeping a cool head. Because of this, these individuals can tolerate nearly any beliefs or views their loved ones have. No matter how these ideals differ from their own, these people are very skilled at putting their differences aside for the sake of their family. These signs are very stubborn, especially when it comes to aspects of their character or behavior. These are very much the type of people to do something simply because someone said not to.

Mercury in Libra

Mercury controls the way we communicate with one another.

People with Mercury in Libra have brilliant judgment because they weigh all possible options before making a decision. Because of this, this individual may have heightened confidence in their decisions and thus express their decisions very clearly and concisely. This individual is careful to listen to all arguments of an issue and point out irregularities before making their own decision. Even once they do make a decision, they occasionally will prefer to say, "Well, I'm kind of in the middle of both ideas," or something to that respect.

Venus in Scorpio

Venus controls how we handle romance and how we appreciate beauty.

Individuals with their Venus in Scorpio are often unafraid of commitment and attract partners with their intensity. The appeal of this sign lies mostly in their dedication and intense loyalty. Relationships with this individual are not for those looking for something fast, fun, and free.

Mars in Cancer

Mars controls the commitment to action and energy.

The combination of this planet and this sign leans this individual towards a passive-aggressive nature. While preferring to handle situations calmly, if these individuals feel cornered, they can be prone to explosive displays of emotion. The strength of these individuals lies in their patience; they prefer to bide their time before an attack to find the perfect timing.

Jupiter in Pisces

Jupiter is in charge of our luck and optimism throughout our lives.

This individual would gain the best fortune when they are giving good to others. Being charitable, devoted, and compassionate is likely to bring good luck into this person's life.

Saturn in Aquarius

Saturn is the source of motivation and how it is used.

This individual will throw themselves into their studies unless their family cannot support it. In this situation, this individual will take up the task themselves and learn all they need on their own in a practical environment. This person is particular and focused on his or her work. They may enjoy spending time with those who have more life experience in order to learn about the world.

Uranus in Virgo

Interested in finding uncommon solutions to problems.

Neptune in Scorpio

Little interest in the superficial. Prefers to be surrounded by practicality.

Pluto in Virgo

Individuals have an easy time collecting information.

Ascendant in Virgo

The Ascendant is an indicator of how someone will act in his or her life; it is a symbol of how others will see you and your attitudes towards life.

Individuals with Virgo rising will often care very little about their appearance. Depending on the people they are with, this individual has a certain shyness that may come off as cool or reserved. These individuals also have an extreme awareness of their bodies; they often are very good at sports that require good body awareness, such as dance, martial arts, or gymnastics. These signs also pay a lot of attention to detail and often notice things in situations that many others would overlook.

The 12 Houses

In addition to all of the previous planetary signs, birth charts also include what is known as "Houses". These houses can be described as sunglasses with differently tinted lenses for each sign. They predict how you will view and experience common life events differently or in comparison with other people. So, while you and another person may be viewing the same event, you may be seeing it very differently due to the sign within that house for you.

Note: The Ascendant takes the spot of the first house, so we will begin at House II.

House II in Virgo

House II represents material values and how one feels about their possessions.

Individuals with the sun in their second house tend to take pride in their possessions and have a strong need for security in life. This person keeps their promises and is very dependable. This person may be impulsive in their spending habits.

House III in Libra

House III is how people prefer to learn and gain knowledge.

These individuals prefer to learn through the telling of stories. They may surround themselves with elders to learn from their life experiences.

House IV in Sagittarius

House IV is how people value family and predict the roots they may set.

This person will most likely fall in love with someone from far away and live their life there with them.

House V in Capricorn

House V is in control of self-expression, entertainment, and gambling.

This individual is very serious and calculates every possibility before making a decision. This person prefers not to take risks.

House VI in Aquarius

House VI predicts how we handle learning through transactions.

This person may have issues with blood circulation.

House VII in Pisces

House VII predicts how the individual handles one-on-one relationships.

This individual may rush into marriage or partnership.

House VIII in Pisces

House VIII is how emotionally secure a person feels.

This individual may have trouble being accountable with difficult subjects such as intimacy, death, or finances. This person may want to avoid such topics but must refrain from doing so.

House IX in Aries

House IX is how learnings affect a person's identity.

This person should take risks while traveling.

House X in Gemini

House X represents the kind of work one will fulfill in their lifetime and becomes very important as they grow old.

This person is most likely to end up in a profession that requires much change and variance throughout the day.

House XI in Cancer

House XI is where this person feels most secure.

This person will maintain lifelong friendships, second only to family.

House XII in Leo

House XII controls this person's experience in education.

This individual may have problems with authority.

You may notice throughout this that some aspects are very well explained while others are only a sentence. This is mostly because a lot of the birth chart overlaps and to do several paragraphs on every part of the birth chart would mean repeating information multiple times. Instead, you are reading the most important differences between each part of the birth chart. There is much more that one can include in a birth chart. In fact, there are whole textbooks devoted to the natal chart by itself. Within this chapter, we have included only the parts that are most important and practical in understanding day-to-day life. In the next chapter, we will go into more detail about how this chart can help you in understanding the people around you.

Chapter 4: The Ascendant and How It Affects Our Daily Actions and Choices

Within this chapter, you will begin to understand how choices you make and actions you take –without even realizing it – may be connected back to your Ascendant. This can also help with understanding the actions of other people and why they may respond to certain situations in certain ways. Within this chapter, we will be focusing on the Rising Zodiac of the birth chart.

The Ascendant

The Ascendant is widely considered one of the most important aspects of our birth chart. With the consideration of the Ascendant, a person's personality can be completely different from what their star sign may suggest. Our Ascendant, or our "Rising" predicts how we handle issues on a day-to-day basis. This sign characterizes our automatic responses to the everyday. Here, we have given a very basic interpretation of how different rising signs may react to their environment. Please remember that an individual's personality is based on far more than these rough estimations.

Aries

The Aries Ascendant prefers to act rather than wait. They tend not to think ahead before rushing forward to complete the task at hand. These individuals are independent and have very little patience for slowness or dilly-dallying. In decision-making scenarios, these individuals may choose the first choice offered to them or the one that would have them reach their goal the fastest. Despite the impatience of this individual, they are always quick to offer a smile.

Taurus

Taurus Ascendants' favorite phrase is "Slow and steady wins the race." Not one to rush through things or make brash decisions, these individuals are highly dependable. These people tend to be resistant to change – being very set in their ways. The first response of a Taurus Ascendant, when faced with a difficult situation, is to feel things out within the world around them. They take in the sights, the smells, and the practical qualities of life. These individuals are highly determined, and as a result, can be rather inflexible.

Gemini

Gemini Rising are often very curious and interested in the social qualities of the people around them. They yearn to learn about the social tendencies of people and may be interested in sociology. These are individuals that ask every question under the sun before making a decision. On occasion, these people focus too much on their mental agility and may forget to show those around them that they care about their well-being. As a result, they can come off as uncaring or unappreciative. Those with air signs will have an easier time understanding these individuals. Gemini Rising individuals love to share their knowledge with those around them and often spend a lot of time explaining things, from theoretical ideals to information about the physical world. Some of these people can make wonderful teachers. Despite their lust for knowledge, this sign in rising can be prone to short attention spans. They may need constant stimulation to stay on track.

Cancer

Cancer Ascendant often has a warm or comfortable air about them. They usually can fit the stereotype of the "Girl next door". These individuals are very sensitive to their environment, and as a result, can get flustered when in public. When faced with difficult situations, these individuals' first instinct is to protect themselves. As a result, they can come off as shy or soft-spoken. In relationships, these individuals like for their partner to be strong and steady. They like to have confidence in their partner's ability to care for them – whether that means emotionally, financially, or physically.

Leo

Leo rising often stand out in a crowd. They give off a certain energy that people around them can't help but notice. Sometimes they are noticed by being loud and boisterous, sometimes they are noticed because of their outward appearance, and other times they just have a sort of magnetism that draws people to them. These individuals can be very self-conscious and are constantly aware of their bodies and what others may be thinking when they look at them. These individuals may feel as though they are on a constant stage. These individuals also have a strong tendency to overestimate just about everything. Living in excess is one of their biggest problems. Leo rising tend to enjoy grand gestures; these are the individuals that will ask someone to marry them on a jumbotron or apologize to someone on a stage in front of hundreds of people.

Virgo

Virgo rising tend to be understated and reserved in their outward appearance and mannerisms. Quite the opposite of Leo rising. When faced with difficult decisions, these individuals prefer to take time to absorb the situation before making a hard decision. Occasionally this quality can make them appear as cold, standoffish people when, in reality, they simply need to learn more about you and the situation first. These individuals are extremely aware of their bodies. They instantly know when something is wrong, and they need to do something about it. Many are very concerned with 'mind body health' and may enjoy spending their time in sports such as yoga or meditation.

Libra

Libra Ascendants are very likable individuals. They tend to come off as kind and fair and easily make many friends. Despite their pleasant demeanor, these individuals often have a long history of messy relationships. They sometimes can be described as a "Serial Monogamist". Any time you talk with one, they are in a new relationship. These individuals are often very careful about how they look; their image is often everything to them. They carefully choose their hairstyle and clothing each morning. These individuals can be alarmingly persuasive and usually make brilliant salespeople or marketing professionals. When faced with a difficult situation, these individuals often try to find their way to a compromise that benefits both parties.

Scorpio

Scorpio rising often have a very commanding or leadership presence about them. Scorpio rising either has a huge group of friends or a wide group of enemies. They don't often go unnoticed; you either love them or hate them. These are very private individuals who like to have a lot of control over their environment. When faced with difficult decisions or situations, these individuals prefer to strategize their actions.

Sagittarius

This rising sign loves adventure and experiencing new things. They often spend the entirety of their lives reaching for goals that are just out of their grasp. Often these individuals don't actually know what they would do if they succeeded in getting the thing they want. These individuals tend to be very restless and constantly on the go. These people love to share their opinions on every subject with everyone. While these individuals aren't always outgoing, they tend to show a sort of security in who they are whether they are shy or not.

Capricorn

Capricorn ascendants often have a very dry sense of humor that gets pulled off perfectly by their serious personality. While these individuals often come off as serious and dry, they can be quite hilarious and unexpected. These are often the type of people to dress for success and succeed as a result. As children, Capricorns are often deemed the responsible ones and usually live up to this verdict. They often adopt a strong sense of tradition and family values at a very young age. These individuals tend to be very concerned about their future and constantly wonder if they are trying hard enough. Success does not come easy to these people, but they tend to gain it through their affinity to hard work. These individuals are often the subject of incredible success stories, are known for having tough childhoods, and have overcome many obstacles in their lives.

Aquarius

Aquarius rising are their own people; they are unique and often possess a very different set of skills and talents from a normal person. A person in this Ascendant is often very proud of their individuality and will work hard to stand out from the crowd. Aquarius rising are often not surprised by life's obstacles; they typically have a lot of life experience and want others to know that they are very experienced. Most Aquarius rising are very likable and kind. These individuals are often known to express their uniqueness through their clothing and usually like to have some surprising or different pieces to set their outfits apart from others.

Pisces

Pisces in rising are often very flexible people who conform to those around them. They tend to be open to everyone and try to make everyone feel included. These individuals are incredibly impressionable and have a soft-hearted disposition about them. Decision making is not these individuals' strong point as they want to include every possible solution to create the best answer. These people like to live freely and can view organization and structure as being too limiting. Physically, these individuals have sensitive bodies – being prone to allergies that come and go as well as an over sensibility to drugs. These individuals often have a soft charm about them that draws people in.

Chapter 5: Tarot Reading – A Brief History of the Art

The origin of Tarot cards coincides with the beginning of everyday playing cards.

The historical version of playing cards as we know them today first originated in ancient Islamic societies.

Over time, these playing cards traveled to Europe and first appeared in 1375. These cards then began to evolve into the Tarot cards we are familiar with today.

In the year 1440, the Duke of Milan sent a letter requesting several decks of "triumph" cards. It was these "Triumph" cards that would eventually evolve into modern-day Tarot.

The origin of Tarot started as a simple card game – this card game was quite different from modern-day card decks. These decks were built with four suits, with cards numbered one through ten and court cards of a queen, king, knight, and page. In addition to these, the decks also contained 22 picture cards.

This game was played in a fashion similar to Bridge and began to be called "Tarrochi" in Italian around the year 1530.

Chapter 6: Tarot Cards – The Different Cards and Their Commonly Used Meanings

Within this chapter, we will explain the different meanings and interpretations of each of the commonly used Tarot cards. A single Tarot card deck typically has about 78 cards in it. These cards are broken into five separate sections – Major Arcana, Cups, Pentacles, Swords, and Wands. The core of a deck of Tarot cards is often considered the "Major Arcana". The Major Arcana is a section of the Tarot deck that, when put in order, follows the life of humanity from origin to the end of all. This section of the deck is very interesting because it tells the story of all of life from beginning to end while also acting as signs or predictors of different things in a person's life. For the sake of this text, we will give brief descriptions of each card from the Major Arcana and what they may mean if pulled in a Tarot Reading. If you are interested in learning about all of the cards of the Tarot deck, we highly recommend visiting the website labyrinthos.co, which has much more information on the subject.

Major Arcana

The Major Arcana is a section of the Tarot deck that contains 22 cards that tell the story of human spiritual evolution. It begins with the Fool and moves through the different stages of life until it reaches the World. One important thing to remember is that Tarot cards have different meanings whether they are upside down or Right-Side Up. We will give a brief explanation of each meaning for each card.

The Fool – Right-Side Up

The Fool is often depicted as a young man walking obliviously towards a cliff. This card typically represents innocence and naiveté. The individual in the image seems to be uncaring of the danger/s that await him. This card is considered number 0 – the number 0 in Tarot is considered a number of potentials. He is often described as a blank slate, not yet having a clear-cut personality but rather preparing to embark on a journey that will shape his experiences and ideals. Broadly speaking, the pulling of the Fool Right-Side Up is indicative of the beginning of a journey. This journey will bring a sense of freedom from life's restraints and difficulties. Each day under this card is considered the beginning of a new adventure with an almost childlike gleam to it. Pulling this card in a reading is typically a call to give into one's riskier side and accept new challenges and opportunities.

The Fool – Upside Down

The Fool being drawn Upside Down typically shows a more negative side of the card. This means that the individual in question may be literally acting like a fool or ignoring obvious signs of danger. This card is often trying to alert the card holder to something that is too good to be true.

The Magician – Right-Side Up

The Magician is a complicated card to understand. It depicts a man pointing at the sky and down towards the ground, a gesture that is often interpreted as meaning "as above so below," which is a phrase used to mean that the earth reflects the heavens. Within this card is also the symbolism of the five suits of the Tarot deck meaning that the Magician holds power to all five elements. This card represents the willpower of an individual and pulling this card Right-Side Up may mean that it is time for one to tap into their full potential.

The Magician – Upside Down

When this card is pulled Upside Down, it may mean that it is time for the card holder to make changes in their life. The reverse Magician card represents an illusion of grandeur. The magic occurring in one's life may be that of deceit and trickery. This card may indicate that there is a person in one's life who appears to have their best interest at heart but, in fact, cares only about themselves.

The High Priestess – Right-Side Up

The High Priestess card typically depicts a woman sitting on a throne between two opposing pillars that represent the opposing forces of reality. Her location between them indicates that she is meant to be the mediator between these two pillars. The High Priestess is often connected with knowledge of the inner mind and pulling her during a reading session can indicate that the card holder should trust their gut over their intellect.

The High Priestess – Upside Down

Pulling the High Priestess Upside Down often indicates that the card holder is having difficulty listening to their intuition. This often means that it may be time to settle down and contemplate their possible options rather than take the logical routes through them. They may also have been ignoring signs from their gut intuition to follow through with the decision. Their actions may feel contradictory to their internal values and beliefs, and they may be feeling confused about their recent decisions. However, in case this card is pulled, one may want to try asking questions about their inner self, which may show that they follow whichever is truer to their internal beliefs and values.

The Empress – Right-Side Up

The Empress card often represents fertility because it depicts a woman sitting on a throne surrounded by beautiful, boundless nature. This woman is believed to be representative of the earth goddess; her world is ruled by Venus which indicates an appreciation of beauty, love, and harmony. Pulling the Empress Right-Side Up shows how deeply we are connected to our femininity. This is often associated with a nurturing characteristic; she may be pulled as a sign to connect more firmly with one's sensuality. One must often compare this card with the others pulled during a reading, but if the other cards are also indicative of it, this card may be a sign of pregnancy. If not, this card can also be a sign of the birth of a new business idea or creative process.

The Empress – Upside Down

Because of the Empress' nurturing tendencies, a large part of this card indicates wanting to care for others. However, pulling this card Upside Down indicates that the card holder has spent too much time caring for others and has thus lost some of their strengths and willpower. They may have begun to neglect their needs either physically or mentally or smothered those they are caring for.

The Emperor – Right-Side Up

The Emperor card is often considered to be the opposite of its predecessor, the Empress. Where the Empress ruled with love care and nurturing, the Emperor is known to rule with force, action, and aggression. This card also represents the wisdom of experience, as shown in the Emperor's long beard. Behind the Emperor, the viewer can see many large mountains that represent his ambition. Pulling this card in a reading may indicate that the person in question is a strong leader and brilliant strategist. This card may also be a sign of strong discipline and strong paternal values, as well as a sign of someone with the rational ideals of a man who knows how to serve his people. For future plans, this card may indicate that they will go through unhindered as long as they approach the plans in the same mindset as the Emperor – methodically and strategically.

The Emperor – Upside Down

This card pulled Upside Down indicates the abuse of power in one's life. This could mean that the card holder is abusing power, or someone else in their life is exerting a power over them that should not have been bestowed upon them. In a personal context, this card upside down can show a lack of self-control and an inability to handle difficult situations.

The Hierophant – Right-Side Up

This card is also known as the Pope or the High Priest. It shows a person of very strong religious connotation. This person is typically shown holding a triple cross, each of the horizontal bars representing the Father, the Son, and the Holy Ghost. At his feet are two acolytes meant to represent the transfer of knowledge from one to another. For the card holder, this sign represents the yearning for a previous structure – that is, the person in question wants to be a part of a society or organization greater than themselves. They may wish to join a clergy or another organization of ancient connotation. This is a sign that straying from traditions or set beliefs is not the way to go.

The Hierophant – Upside Down

The Hierophant pulled Upside Down may indicate that one is feeling too constrained by the structures and rules in their life. This means that they may be tempted to try unorthodox approaches to traditional results. In children, this may be a sign that they are about to hit a rebellious streak or feel resentful of smothering parents.

The Lovers – Right-Side Up

The Lovers card shows an angel blessing a couple. The couple appears to be safe and happy in what is assumed to be the Garden of Eden. This card has a sense of harmony and balance unparalleled by any other. When pulled, this can indicate a very strong relationship between two individuals. Sometimes it can show two individuals being joined in marriage, but it can also represent a strong relationship of friendship or kin. Another meaning that is often overlooked is the burden of choices. This could mean that the card holder needs to focus more on a dilemma facing them at that moment. On a more personal level, this card can mean that they are in the process of understanding and discerning their belief system outside of societal norms.

The Lovers – Upside Down

Pulling this card Upside Down indicates that one is dealing with multiple conflicts that can either be internal or external. There is a lack of balance and harmony in one's life that is creating pressure and strife in their relationships. They may consider pinpointing the root of the issue and why they are punishing themselves and the people around them for it. Another interpretation of this card is a recent break or loss of strong communication with another person. This may be causing an imbalance between the card holder and those around them. Finally, this card can also indicate that one is avoiding taking responsibility for their actions. This means that they may need to try and let go of their pride and take responsibility for their recent decisions.

The Chariot – Right-Side Up

This card has very strong celestial connotations in its artwork. It depicts a man sitting in a cart being pulled by a black and a white sphinx. Above the man's head is a canopy of blue with white stars, meant to represent the heavens. Adorning his shoulders are two crescent moons representing his spiritual influence and power. The coloring of the sphinxes is rather important as it represents the opposing forces that the man must learn to work with and turn towards a common goal. Pulling this card in a reading is a sign that one may have difficult challenges ahead but that if they maintain a focused and confident demeanor, they will overcome them and be a much greater person for it. It also indicates that the quest they are about to embark on may cause them to display behavior they have never shown before. They may be surprised by their skills and abilities.

The Chariot – Upside Down

Pulling this card Upside Down indicates that the card holder lacks some level of willpower or focus. They may have "driven off course" so to speak and probably need to take some time to collect themselves and attempt to find the road again. This card can also mean that they lack control and are taking certain things lying down when it may be in their best interest to fight for their independence. It should be seen as a wake-up call that they need to get their head in the game and start pushing forward harder than ever before.

The Strength – Right-Side Up

This is a particularly interesting card – as its name suggests – because it would usually represent traditional power and strength; however, the artwork depicts a woman of a delicate demeanor calmly holding the jaws of a lion shut. The lion is drawn with all the characteristics of a strong, powerful beast and as an interesting dynamic, the woman looks perfectly peaceful as she holds his mouth shut. This shows an interesting idea of strength that is somewhat uncommon in ancient contexts. The interpretation of this is that strength is not in physical prowess but in the calm mental courage that someone with immense love and compassion can contain. Pulling this card in a reading session often indicates that one contains a sort of inner strength that they may be unaware of. It shows that they excel at maintaining a calm demeanor and attitude in the face of distress. This card also shows that the person in question is very patient and can utilize that patience to achieve anything they set their mind to.

The Strength – Upside Down

Pulling this card Upside Down indicates that the card holder may be lacking certain qualities that would benefit them in upcoming trials and tribulations. It is a sign that they may be unsure of themselves and that an upcoming challenge is going to uproot their very belief system. This can also indicate mental depression as it may be predicting a loss of passion for things one normally cares very deeply about. The drawing of this card can also predict that a person may withdraw from traditional society in the coming months. This person may have difficulty including themselves in social events or activities. They may want to consider watching out for these signs in the coming months and having their mental health watched by a professional.

The Hermit – Right-Side Up

This card has some very interesting contradictions in its artwork. The image on this card typically depicts an elderly man holding a lantern atop a tall snowy mountain. The mountain, in this case, represents accomplishment and success. What is interesting is that the old man looks disheveled and broken, not at all satisfied with his accomplishment, but appears to have gained a great amount of wisdom. He is also holding a large walking staff which represents power but can also be interpreted as a sign that his mission is not complete, that he now needs to share his knowledge and experience with the rest of the world. Pulling this card may mean that the person in question needs to take some time for themselves to reflect upon life and the many experiences they have had. This individual may be considering going about life alone – whatever that may mean to them if it involves a partner or a friend, they may be considering leaving that individual. This card is not meant to sway that person either way but to let them know that they may need to think a while before making a decision.

The Hermit – Upside Down

When pulled Upside Down, the person in question may be certain that they would like to traverse the world alone but should consider that doing so may be harmful to themselves or others. This card also denotes the dangers of looking within. It reminds the viewer that while self-reflection is good and necessary, if they are not careful, they may find themselves in the throes of madness. In the professional realm, this card upside down indicates that one may be about to get to the bottom of a problem that has been bothering them for a long time.

The Wheel of Fortune – Right-Side Up

The Wheel of Fortune card is the most symbolically packed card in the deck. It is full of images of symbolic significance and religiously charged actions. At the very center of the card is an image of a wheel surrounded by different beings that represent four signs of the Zodiac, the Angel, the Eagle, the Bull, and the Lion. These beings represent Leo, Taurus, Scorpio, and Aquarius. Each of these creatures is holding a text that is meant to represent the Torah, a symbol of infinite wisdom. This card also contains a snake that represents the act of descending into the material world, as well as a sphinx and what appears to be a type of devil or Anubis. These last two are said to represent the power of the gods and kings as well as the underworld. Pulling this card in a reading may mean that one needs to recognize that some things in life are out of their control and that the wheel of life continues to turn no matter their actions.

The Wheel of Fortune – Upside Down

When this card is pulled Upside Down, it often indicates misfortune and bad luck following the person in question. As grim as this sounds, the inclusion of the wheel points out that this luck will eventually turn as all things do. One must make sure to release control and be comfortable in the fact that the luck will turn their way given time.

Justice – Right-Side Up

The symbolism of this card is quite clear in the imagery. This card is full of symbolism pointing to law, truth, and fairness of the soul. The woman of Justice sits in a throne holding a set of scales in one hand and a sword in the other. The scales are said to represent the balance of intuition and logic while the double-edged sword is said to represent fairness. On her crown is a square that is meant to represent clarity. Pulling this card Right-Side Up in a reading session indicates that one's decisions at a current time hold great importance for their future. This also indicates that their actions or the actions of those around them may be judged by the universe soon. This may be shown in the revelation of a truth kept secret or a wrong that may be corrected.

Justice – Upside Down

This card Upside Down has many interpretations. One of those is that the card holder may be in denial of their actions or the consequences of their actions. This often means that they need to let the past go and try to move forward. Accepting the decisions of the universe will help them continue their life without hindrance.

The Hanged Man – Right-Side Up

This card depicts a man hanging upside down from a tree. Within this card, we see one huge contradiction that points to the symbolism of the card. While this man is suspended in a way that should be uncomfortable, the man seems to be without any worry, with his second foot free and his arms held casually behind his back. The tree he is hanging from is meant to represent the living world with its roots down in the underworld and the branches holding up the heavens. Because of the calm expression on the man's face, it is believed that he is hanging by his own free will. He wears red pants to represent humanity's passion and vitality. The blue in his shirt represents the calm serenity of his emotions. Pulling this card in a reading indicates that the viewer may be in a situation that is not the best or most comfortable but needs to understand that this time is a sacrifice necessary to progress further in life. This may show that they are in a time of indecision and may be an indicator that they need to postpone actions that are time sensitive in order to make a better, more informed decision.

The Hanged Man – Upside Down

The reversal of this card has very specific connotations that are somewhat rare in the deck of Tarot. This card in reverse indicates that the person in question is wasting their time on something and receiving nothing in return. This is a sign that they may be stuck and need to consider switching up their methods of handling life. There may be something in their life that they are devoting a lot of time to that is not worth the effort anymore.

Death – Right-Side Up

This card depicts Death as a skeleton riding a white horse in full armor holding a flag with white designing. Death drawn as a skeleton wearing armor represents that bones are the only thing left after one perishes, but that death is impenetrable. The white horse Death rides represents the purity of death as everyone is purified upon leaving this world. Beneath Death lies the dead bodies of individuals from all classes – a king, a pauper, a woman, and a child. Death is a very misunderstood card in the Tarot deck. Often feared, this card has a much deeper meaning than simply death and pain. Rather than the ending of life, this card can also mean the ending of a phase in one's life to give way for something new and more exciting. It is a sign that one needs to begin putting their focus into what lies ahead of them rather than what they have been doing. Another interpretation is that they may be going through a major change or transition in their life.

Death – Upside Down

This card flipped Upside Down means about the same thing as the card Right-Side Up but with an added connotation. It still indicates that one may be experiencing a great change in their life, but now it also includes the fact that they may be denying or resisting it. If a person pulls this card, they may want to consider a decision that they have turned down multiple times and may be willed to try it out. Whether this is in a romantic sense or the sense of a new sport or club. They may be denying themselves change out of fears of the unknown and should consider accepting the fact that life moves on and there is no way to stop change.

Temperance – Right-Side Up

The symbolism of this card very strongly represents unity among opposites. This card depicts an angel without defining sexual characteristics, which hints that the sexes are in perfect balance. In addition, this angel has one foot in the water and one on land, which shows the connection of the material world to the subconscious. She also has a square inscribed on her robe with a triangle in the middle. This represents the connection between the clarity of the physical world (the square) and the spiritual realm of the Father, Son, and the Holy Ghost (the triangle). She holds two cups with water flowing infinitely between them representing infinite unity. Pulling this card shows that one is a person who remains calm and balanced in the face of uncertainty. This card indicates a sense of clarity and that one knows what they want in life and love. This may also indicate that it may be time to look through previous decisions and choices and attempt to balance them out with other options in one's life.

Temperance – Upside Down

Pulling this card in reverse is a sign that something in the card holder's life is unbalanced and needs to be reconsidered. They may also be lacking in a long-term goal or vision of the future, which may be causing some internal turmoil and a lack of purpose. They may also be suffering in excess. The Temperance card serves as a reminder that everything is only good in moderation and that to live a happy life, one must be careful not to devote too much in their life to one thing or individual.

The Devil – Right-Side Up

This card shows the Devil in his stereotypical satyr form. The Devil, in addition to being half-goat and half-man, also has an inverted pentagram on his forehead as well as bat wings adorning his back.

Beneath him are a nude woman and a nude man chained together, a feature which shows that the Devil has dominion over them. Both humans have goat-like characteristics which show that the longer they spend in the Devil's world, the more they leave their human selves. Receiving this card in a reading session is very grim, indeed. It shows that one may be feeling entrapped, empty, or lacking in fulfillment. It also indicates they may have become a slave to their material possessions. They may know already that they are heading down a slippery slope but may feel powerless to stop their fall. This may also indicate a possible addiction to substances or material pleasures.

The Devil – Upside Down

This card being pulled Upside Down indicates a much more positive reading. It represents breaking free from the chains that may be binding one metaphorically. The downside to this, of course, is that breaking these chains and changing these habits is not easy and may come with a price. One has to be prepared when pulling this card to endure extreme hardship to come out better. Often when this card is pulled, it is recommended that the person in question take some time to self-reflect and perhaps even write a list of all of the habits they need to change.

The Tower – Right-Side Up

This card shows a tall, foreboding tower that has been struck by lightning and is set ablaze as a result. As their final act, several people are leaping from the windows of this burning tower. It is often believed that these individuals are the same two individuals that we see in The Devil card. This tower represents ambition that is built on faulty principle and as a result, must be destroyed in order to create something new. The pulling of this card in a reading is a sign of necessary but also very difficult change. This often means that a complete uproot is necessary to move forward in life. This can mean the destruction of a relationship that has turned sour or the physical change of location from one home to another.

The Tower – Upside Down

Pulling this card in reverse is often a sign that great catastrophe is headed in one's direction. This may mean that something they cut corners with in the beginning is about to resurface and they will have to suffer the consequences of their actions. This may indicate that they need to become more self-reliant in order to rebuild a new foundation of better quality.

The Star – Right-Side Up

This card shows a nude woman kneeling at the edge of a pond. She is holding two cups of water, one she is using to nourish the ground and one is being poured out into the pond. Above her is one large star with seven smaller stars surrounding it. Pulling this card in a reading is a message to remind the viewer that they contain many great gifts blessed to them. This card indicates that they may be doubting their gifts because of recent traumatic events (The Tower). This card is meant as a reminder to trust in one's abilities and be grateful for the gifts they are blessed with.

The Star – Upside Down

Pulling this card Upside Down indicates that one is feeling overwhelmed by the challenges facing them. They may feel as though the entire world is conspiring against them and there is nothing they can do to stop it. This card serves as a reminder to nurture hope for the future and try to find the root of what is making one feel so defeated.

The Moon – Right-Side Up

The Moon card serves as a lesson in duality for the receiver. Upon the card is a scene that depicts a road flanked by two animals, a civilized family dog and a ferocious wild wolf. As the road goes into the distance, it is perfectly in the middle of two towers and goes straight down the middle of a great mountain. The two towers are supposed to represent good and evil, and their similar appearance serves as a reminder that evil actions and people can look the same as ones of good intentions. This card can be interpreted as a representation of an illusion; something in the viewer's life is not as it seems.

The Moon – Upside Down

Pulling this card Upside Down often indicates some level of confusion in one's life. This may mean that there is some sort of progress they want to make but do not know how to proceed. They may want to consider consulting someone who is an expert in the area they are confused about. This card can also mean that one's feelings of confusion are beginning to dissipate.

The Sun – Right-Side Up

This card represents life and the optimism of childhood. In this card, a nude child is riding a white horse underneath a bright sun with flowers framing him. The white horse is a symbol of the purity of the child and the fact that he is nude shows he has nothing to hide for he has not yet learned of shame or modesty. Pulling this card Right-Side Up has extremely positive implications. This card is a sign of success, radiance, and strength in the individual who has pulled it.

The Sun – Upside Down

Pulling this card Upside Down often means that the viewer has difficulty seeing the positive side to life. This individual may be cynical and only see clouds in the sunlight. This might be hindering their confidence and making it more difficult to succeed in life. This card can also be interpreted as meaning they are being unrealistic about something.

Judgment – Right-Side Up

This card is drawn in mind of what the final Judgement Day would look like in a religious sense. It shows an angel, assumedly Gabriel, giving his trumpet call and men and women rising from their graves to respond. They hold out their arms ready to be judged. Pulling this card in a reading indicates that one may be about to enter a time of self-reflection. They are about to enter a time in their life in which they will be evaluating their past decisions and actions. This card can also mean they are in a period of awakening. They may have a clear idea of what needs to be changed in order to become a better version of themselves.

Judgement – Upside Down

Pulling this card in reverse means that the card holder may be too harsh of a judge upon themselves. It is this judgement that may have caused them to miss opportunities in the past because they doubted their ability to rise to the challenge. This card can also be a sign that they may need to take a step back and review their life up to this point. They may also be focusing too hard on their past decisions and not allowing themselves to move forward in life.

The World – Right-Side Up

As the final card in the Major Arcana section of the Tarot deck, this card is full of beautiful symbolism. In the center of the card is a woman dancing with a sash lying loosely around her body. She holds a wand in either hand and has a pleasant expression on her face. Surrounding her is a green wreath with ribbons tied around them. In each of the four corners of the card are the same four Zodiac symbols from the Wheel of Fortune card – Scorpio, Leo, Taurus, and Aquarius. The woman in the center of this card represents balance and evolution's constant and dynamic motion through time. The wreath surrounding her represents success while the ribbons are tied in infinity symbols and reflect as such. The Zodiacs represent the four elements, the four corners of the universe, and the four evangelicals. When combined, all of these symbols represent balance and unity. To pull this card in a reading indicates a reaching of enlightenment or finding the perfect balance within a person's life. Being the last card in the Major Arcana line gives it an additional meaning. That is, it also represents completion and is a sign that one's hard work is beginning to pay off. In daily life, this may mean the completion of schooling, such as a graduation, or it may mean being able to retire with a healthy retirement sum.

The World – Upside Down

Pulling this card in reverse still indicates that one is reaching the end of something. The difference now is that this end may be bittersweet. They may be looking back, feeling unfinished in this chapter that is closing. They may be regretting not trying hard enough or giving enough chances to do something. They may be feeling a sort of emptiness they have not felt before.

As you can see, the Major Arcana series has very strong symbolical implications that can easily be connected to the human experience. Each of these cards represents events or stages in an individual's life, as well as the events in humanity's walk on this earth, both of which reflect one another. It is this reason that is considered the core of the Tarot deck with the other sections as more of flavors or accents to be placed upon these cards. These other cards are very important as they can change the veil that one sees themselves through, but they do not make up the core, most basic events, and ideals of a person's life.

Chapter 7: Tarot, The Star Signs and How They Work Together

It may come as a surprise to some (and not to others) that Zodiac Astrology and Tarot card reading are very closely related. Each of the Major Arcana cards is connected to a star sign and often have traits relating to that sign. Similarly, to the Zodiac, each of the Tarot card "suits" are separated into different elemental classifications as well – a byproduct of being connected so closely with the Zodiac. These elements are where we will begin to pull our comparisons from. The suit of a Tarot deck loosely shows what the cards within that suit predict and describe within a person's life. The elements and their attached suits and Zodiac are as follows:

- Fire – Suit of Wands
    - i) Associated with action, power, and willfulness
    - ii) Zodiac: Aries, Leo, Sagittarius
- Water – Suit of Cups
    - i) Associated with creativity, emotion, and connection to the environment
    - ii) Zodiac: Cancer, Scorpio, Pisces
- Air – Suit of Swords

i) Associated with intelligence, communication, and progress
  ii) Zodiac: Gemini, Libra, Aquarius
- Earth – Suit of Pentacles
  i) Associated with dependability, practicality, and problems of the body
  ii) Taurus, Virgo, Capricorn

In addition to the elements, each court card and Zodiac sign is also organized by a system known as "Modalities". The sections of this system are known as Cardinal Signs, Fixed signs, and Mutable Signs. These are broken down for you below:

- Cardinal
  i) Queens
  ii) Signs under this modality are known for being decisive and initiating big decisions
  iii) Aries-Fire
  iv) Cancer-Water
  v) Libra-Air
  vi) Capricorn-Earth
- Fixed
  i) Knights
  ii) Signs under this modality are known for being dependable, stable, and down to earth
  iii) Taurus-Earth
  iv) Leo-Fire
  v) Scorpio-Water
  vi) Aquarius-Air
- Mutable
  i) Kings
  ii) Signs under this modality are known for being flexible, creative, and emotional
  iii) Gemini-Air
  iv) Virgo-Earth
  v) Sagittarius-Fire

vi) Pisces-Water

Each of these systems is only recommendations and ideas for how to interpret a deck of Tarot cards relating to the Zodiac. They are in no way set in stone or the rules of the Tarot world.

Interpretation of Tarot and the Zodiac as Guides

So, you've read this far, and maybe you're thinking to yourself, *Oh my goodness, this is so much information. How could this possibly represent me?!* Well, if so, you're right. This is a lot of information, and this doesn't even cover half of what a professional in this subject needs to know. But don't worry – it isn't gospel. The ideas represented in all of these various systems and artwork are only suggestions. They are meant to be tiny parts that work together to suggest what makes up you as an individual. The Tarot, in particular, is meant to be a guide, a helping hand of sorts – there to offer opinion and suggestion but not to tell you what is and isn't true. The Zodiac helps an individual understand who they are and how they handle given situations. Tarot helps to predict the likelihood of situations and to understand why you may be feeling certain ways at certain stages of your life. It is important to take on board both of these pieces of information when making informed decisions regarding your life. A huge theme in the world of Astrology is the idea of balance, of opposites coming together to create the perfect balance. Tarot and Astrology complement each other, giving to this balance in order to create a more balanced life for an individual. The idea here is that for an individual to live a truly happy and successful life, they must have balance. This is why consideration of both Tarot and the Zodiac is vital for the interpretation of a human personality and life. Humans are incredibly complicated, and as such, it makes sense that subjects such as Astrology, which attempts to understand the human mind and human spirit, would also be incredibly complicated. To help you understand this, you must take into account both of these subjects.

In the next chapter, we are going to bring to light a very different method of understanding a person's personality. While this next method is very different from the other methods we have discussed, it does connect to them in an astrological sense.

Chapter 8: Numerology – What Is It and Where Does It Come from?

If you've read the famous *Harry Potter* series, then you know that Hermione's favorite subject is called "Arithmancy" and how it is a subject about the magical qualities of numbers. What you may not know is that this subject is based on a real form of divinity known as "Numerology". Numerology, in reality, is based on the idea that every number has its own vibration. It is this vibration that gives each number different characteristics and affects our lives in different ways. The core of Numerology believes that nothing in the universe happens by coincidence or accident, but rather, it is the vibrational energy of numbers that cause things to happen a certain way. The historical influences of Numerology go as far back as the Greeks with the creation of Pythagoras Numerology by the one and only Pythagoras himself. In addition to the creation of the Pythagorean theorem, Pythagoras was infatuated with the idea of the vibrational frequency of numbers. Pythagoras subscribed to the idea that numbers connect all things – a revelation that began with the discovery that adding up odd numbers beginning with one will always result in a square number. After this revelation, Pythagoras continued his research by studying the mathematical ideals of Arabic, Druid, Phoenician, Egyptian, and Essene sciences.

It is his subject of Numerology that we will be focusing on today, as it is the most widely used and considered. Pythagoras was a brilliant man who formulated ideas that are still widely used and acknowledged today, but he was also incredibly secretive. He taught a school in Crotona, Italy, called the "semi-circle" and was treated more like a secret society. With Pythagoras forbidding his students from writing his teachings, it makes it difficult today to research him as very few of his original writings still exist. However, this wasn't the only secret society devoted to Numerology. In fact, we now know today that Numerology had a hand in many secret societies. From Masons to Rosicrucians, the study and belief of numbers having a deeper connection to the world are highly valued. While Pythagoras paved the way to our modern-day Numerology, he was not the sole creator. Not by several thousands of years.

It is widely debated on who or which community created Numerology first, but what is very interesting is that they all seem to have come to the numerological conclusion on their own. Many ancient societies have their own versions of Numerology, and all of them developed it without truly communicating their ideas to one another. The earliest records we know of today trace back to very early Egypt and Babylon, but we also have evidence that very early in Chinese, Roman, and Japanese history, Numerology was studied and used. In fact, in early Rome, in the year 370 AD, St Augustine of Hippo wrote in a public journal, "Numbers are the Universal language offered by the deity to humans as confirmation of the truth." Of course, at the time, this was a violation of the Roman Church – and as a result, this belief in numbering systems to explain the universe began to disappear.

In the modern age of Numerology, there is a different person who is credited with bringing Numerology out of its cave and into the public eye. Her name is Dr. Julia Stenton, and she is credited with the resurfacing of Numerology in modern-day studies. In fact, she coined the term "Numerology" for a study of names connected with numbers that had previously been unlabeled. Stenton came to this term by combining the Greek word for 'Numerus' or 'Number' and 'Logia' to mean thought or expression.

Numerology has very interesting connections to Tarot and the Zodiac as each of these methods of divination have numbers assigned to them in different ways. The Zodiac, for instance, has a number associated with each of the star signs depending upon its order in the Zodiac lineage. Each Tarot card also has a number associated with it that has a deeper meaning than just its location within the deck. Because of the numbering on each of the Tarot cards, they each have their own distinct meaning within Numerology that gives even more depth to the already very complicated understanding of each card. The number one, for instance, is often associated with new beginnings or the start of something – and there are five cards in a deck of Tarot that are numbered one. These are the Magician card, the Swords, the Ace of Wands, and the Pentacles. And while all of these cards have very different distinct meanings, they all connect in some way to beginnings and fresh starts. People often think of Tarot and Numerology as a cycle, with even numbers typically being sturdy and dependable while odd numbers usually represent some sort of state change or transition. Because of this cyclicity, many numbers can often have multiple meanings, as the end of one thing can mean the beginning of another.

Numerology's connection to the Zodiac is very interesting and not as obvious as its connection with Tarot. While the connection with Tarot is right in front of your face on the cards, Numerology's connection to Astrology lies in the action behind understanding Astrology itself. In order to understand or create someone's birth chart, you must consult their birthdate and time – all numerical values that have great importance in that person's life. In addition, you must then consult the constellations, which you need to know different degrees and longitudinal and latitudinal information about in order to understand fully.

At the base of all of this information is numbers that play a huge part in understanding the personality and inner self of a person. Astrology, while appearing at first glance to be mental and not based in the physical realm, is in fact based very strongly in mathematics and science. Within Numerology itself, each number from zero to nine is ruled by a planet much like the Zodiac in Astrology. It is often when doing a reading of a person that the individual will take both their Zodiac and numerical value into play as each depends and informs one another about the person.

In the next chapter, you will learn how to calculate your numerical values and what each of them mean for you as well as some real-life examples of how your numerology can affect you with certain situations and times.

Chapter 9: Your Numerology – How to Calculate It and What It Means

In the Pythagorean theory of Numerology, it is believed that every individual has five core numbers that make up who they are and how they experience the world. These five numbers are known as the Personality Number, Life Path Number, Expression Number, Heart's Desire Number, and Birth Day Number. All of these numbers are crucial to understanding your Numerology and will organize how you learn about Numerology within this chapter. We will begin with your Personality Number.

Personality Number

In Pythagorean Numerology, every letter in the alphabet is given a corresponding number from one to nine, beginning with the letter A, which equals one, and going through to the letter J, where it starts over at one and repeats through the rest of the alphabet. The personality number, in particular, is calculated by looking at every consonant within someone's full name and giving each of them their corresponding number.

Below is an example name:

Anna Katherina Branden

5 5 2   2 8 9 5   2 9 5 4 4

Now, you will take the numbers from the first name and add them together.

5 + 5 = 10

You will do this separately with the middle name.

2+2+8+9+5= 26

Finally, you will also do this with the last name.

2+9+5+4+5=25

Now you have your three separate numbers from the first, middle, and last name. Now, you will take these numbers that are most likely double digits and will add together the individual numbers in those double-digit numbers until you get to a number between one and nine.

1+0= 1

2+6= 8

2+5=7

Note: It is important to remember that when you come across a number such as 11 or 22, you have found what is called a "Master Number" and do not need to reduce those any further. This also applies to the number 12. They have their own significance and stand on their own as defining numbers.

Now you will add those three separate numbers together.

1+8+7=16

And once again reduce it.

1+6 = 7

7

Now you have a complete personality number! This person has the personality number seven, which you can learn more about later in this chapter. Below, we have included some more calculations for common names.

Emily Elizabeth Smith

4 3   3 8 2 28 14 28

4+3= 7

3+8+2+2+8=23

1+4+2+8=15

7=7

2+3=5

1+5=6

7+5+6=18

1+8=9

9

Now that you know how to calculate your personality number, you've learned *one* out of five of what you need to know your personal Numerology reading. Next, you will learn how to calculate your Heart's Desire Number and what this number affects.

Same as with the Personality number, we are going to start with the connection between our name and the corresponding numbers according to Pythagorean numerology. The difference is where as before you took the number value of the consonants, now you are going to take the number value of the vowels within your name.

Note: Y is a vowel in a word in that it makes sense to replace it with the letter I. For example, with names such as Karyn or Bryan, the y is a vowel, but if the y is accompanied by a vowel already, then it is a consonant. For instance, in words such as 'year', 'yes', or 'yank', in which a vowel is present right next to the y and said y can't really be replaced with anything, the y is a consonant.

An example is given below:

Anna Katherina Branden

1 1   1 5 9 1   1 5

Once again, we will add these together within the different names.

1+1= 2

1+5+9+1= 16

1+5=6

Now we need to reduce the double-digit numbers.

1+6=7

Now we add together the three numbers we are left with.

2+6+7=15

And reduce that number.

5+1=6

6

Now we have reached the Heart's Desire Number, which for this individual is six. The Heart's Desire Number is meant to represent what the individual in question desires or values the most in their life. This can be dreams or ideals for the future. It can also be an indicator of what sort of things motivate them as a person. This number can show what sort of styles they may have or what they prefer to keep in their surrounding environment. Now you know *two* out of five of what you need to understand your personal Numerology. Hold on to these numbers as we will give explanations of their meaning later in this chapter, but for now, get ready to learn the third type of important number: the Expression Number.

The Expression Number

The Expression number in a person dictates what an individual's talents may be. It also can reveal their weaknesses. More specifically, this number is a reflection of the skills and abilities they had when their soul entered their body – the day they were born. The numbers that we found previously show how those skills and abilities develop over time and how one learns to cope in this world with what they were given at birth.

To find an Expression Number, you are going to use the same numbering system as before, but this time, you are going to give a number to every letter within the name, not just the vowels or consonants.

An example is given below:

Anna Katherina Branden

1551 212859951 2915455

Now we will add these numbers as we have done previously.

1+5+5+1=12

2+1+2+8+5+9+9+5+1=42

2+9+1+5+4+5+5=31

Once again, we will add together any double numbers.

4+2=6

3+1=4

2+1=3

Now we add together the three numbers we are left with.

6+4+3=13

Reduce again.

3+1=4

4

Hence, for this individual, we have found that four is their Expression Number. So the traits and skills associated with the number four are what this individual was born with, and their skills are changed and developed differently throughout their life based on the Heart's Desire Number and the Personality Number we figured out before. Now you know *three* out of five of what you need to understand your personal Numerology. Now, we will move on to the second to the last number that is necessary for good numerological reading. Keep the previous numbers you have found for the end of this chapter, as we will give insight on each of the numbers for each section and you will be able to understand your Numerology reading.

Life Path Number

The Date of your birth has, as we have seen, astronomical implications. Nearly every Astrology subsection has some sort of connection to the date of birth as a predictor of the individual. Numerology is no different as we have now reached what is often considered the most important number included in Numerology and is based on your birth date, the Life Path Number. The Life Path Number represents many very important aspects of your life. It represents all of the possibilities and options and challenges you will most likely face in your lifetime. This number is an indicator of the beginning of something magnificent (you), and as such, is often treated as the beginning to a road forked in a million directions. As is insinuated in the name of the number, this number is an indicator of what "Path" you may take in your life and how it will branch off into more and more paths.

To calculate a Life Path Number, you are going to start with the month of a birthdate. Every month is assigned with a number, and you will use this number. If the month is November, you will use 1, and if the month is December, you will reduce 12 to 3.

An example is given below:

March 20, 1999

March – 3

Now we add together the digits in the day.

2+0= 2

Now, finally, we add together the individual digits of the year.

1+9+9+9=28

We will reduce any double-digit numbers.

2+8=10

1+0=1

1

Now we are left with three one-digit numbers, 3, 2, and 1.

You will now add these three numbers together and reduce again if necessary.

3+2+1=6

6

This individual's Life Path Number is six.

Now you know *four* out of five of what you need to understand your personal Numerology. Now that we understand how to calculate the Life Path Number, we have almost reached the end of the calculations – whew! Math is certainly not the most fun part of Astrology, but don't worry – we only have one more number to calculate before we can put together all of our numbers to help understand ourselves as individuals.

Birth Day Number

Your birthday has a very strong value in the world of Numerology. This number requires the least amount of math to understand compared to the other significant numbers. This number only requires the day that you are born, so if you are born on days one-nine, you're done! For every other number, you simply have to add together the two numbers in the date.

Examples are given below:

March 20, 1999

2+0

2

July 16, 1888

1+6

7

This number is a little bit different from the other numbers as the numbers that go into creating the final number are also considered to be quite important. They often compliment or coincide with the final numbers' meaning. Now, you know all *five* of your core number values. Keep them in mind because for the next section of this chapter, as we will be explaining the common traits or meanings behind these numbers.

Your Personality Number One to 12

One

The fact that this number is the first in the series of Personality Numbers is fitting. This number is often associated with traits meant for those who are the firsts. That is, this number is associated with individuals who want to be the first to do anything. They want to be the first female president, the first to design a flying plane, etc.... These individuals are trailblazers and like to control their outcomes. They like to be their own advisors and walk their own path in life.

Two

This number is often associated with traits connected with kindness and softness of the soul. These individuals may often come across as warm and inviting to others around them. These people tend to be well groomed and look nice but also comfortable in their clothes. These individuals are often very passionate and tend to put all they can into their own wellbeing and health as well as their daily work.

Three

Having this number makes someone more likely to be extremely attractive. This number is often associated closely with beauty and grace. People often find the person to be charming and energetic; they exude a sort of magnetism that people cannot deny when they are around them. These individuals can also tend to be extremely romantic, almost to a fault. They fall into passionate, romantic love but then may fall out of that love just as quickly. Good luck and opportunity seem to follow individuals of this number – and as a result, they should be inclined to put themselves out there and not be afraid to try new things.

Four

Four is often associated with traits such as dependability, trust, and stability. People often go to these individuals for their personal judgment on sensitive matters. These individuals can be very helpful in sorting through difficult decisions. People often have an inclination to respect them. They may put off an air of significance, of someone who is meant to be in charge, whether they are or not. These individuals are people who appreciate quality over quantity but can balance the nice things for a good bargain.

Five

Individuals with this number are often very energetic and noticeable in a party. People often appreciate this person's sense of humor and love being around them. Their demeanor often makes those around them feel comfortable and relax. Their optimism spreads to those around them. Unfortunately, they tend to be self-indulgent, mostly within the physical realm. They may have an urge to want to try everything, from food to drugs and sex. Individuals with this number tend to be very charming.

Six

Individuals with this number are extremely empathetic and feel very strong compassion for those around them. As a result, these individuals tend to attract those most in need of a shoulder to cry on. Because of this, it is imperative for these individuals to guard their own emotions very closely as they could begin to confuse another's emotions for their own. Individuals such as these can be very easy to manipulate, especially in the monetary realm as they are subject to others pain. As a result, it is extremely important that individuals with this number stay on guard when someone is telling them their financial problems. These individuals are extremely loyal, and as a result, often end up marrying young and being brilliant parents.

Seven

Individuals with this number are often labeled "mysterious". This is mostly due to their level of independence and self-sufficiency that sets them apart from other numbers. These individuals also tend to be very spiritually inclined; they may have some very strong religious or spiritual beliefs that they care deeply about. They often have very unique insights on life and theology. Because of the mysterious nature of this number, people may have a hard time approaching these individuals as they may come across as intimidating.

Eight

Individuals with this number have a very strong sense of inner strength. This inner strength will be their greatest strength as well as their greatest weakness. Their fortitude can help them in business transactions as well as in navigating difficult situations in their life.

Unfortunately, this also means that their words have extreme power. They may not realize it, but their words carry enough weight to ruin relationships around them. Individuals with this number would also benefit from knowing that they need to be more mindful of their appearance. They often don't realize that the role their wardrobe can play in controlling the room around them is huge, and to dress to impress is very important.

Nine

This number is most commonly associated with artists as well as musicians and other creative geniuses. This is because those with this number are known for being very confident in their abilities and themselves. These individuals very easily win over the admiration of those around them for the practice they put into their skills and work. The downside to this, of course, is that their talent can spur jealousy in those around them. People may accuse them of being arrogant, and they'd be right unless they can focus their power on maintaining a grounded stance in life.

11

Individuals under this number are known for being shy, quiet creatures that have many small nervous ticks. Nail biting is usually cited as one of the most common. These people are typically extremely intuitive and tend to be very vulnerable in most relationships. These individuals often approach life with good intentions but may attract more demanding and predatory personalities. People tend to try and get something out of them because they know that they are more sensitive than others. Because of their gentle and caring nature, people around them may tend to unload their problems on to them. To avoid this, it would be in their best interest to nonverbally convey some level of confidence, either through their clothes, hair, or even just the way they walk. They tend to greatly dislike conflict and often find themselves being named the "peacekeeper" due to their swift compromising tendencies. Being caught in a dispute or argument can often drain them of energy and can be difficult for them to bounce back from.

12/22

The 12th number of Personality Numbers is not, in fact, 12 but 22. This number has very similar but much more extreme traits to number 11. Similarly, to the number 11, these individuals tend to allow themselves to be too vulnerable and may be in danger of being taken advantage of because of it. But because of the power of this number, these individuals are not only in danger of having their material possessions taken advantage of but their emotions as well. These individuals may attract people who thrive off of others pain and misery, or more realistically, those that feel better when other people feel worse. An example of this would be a child that is very sad in their heart picking on another child to make them feel sad as well. The child believes that through hurting the other child, it will make them feel better – when it doesn't in reality. People will often refer to these individuals for their good judgment in difficult situations. These individuals are very responsible with their money and time. They understand the value of a dollar and try to finish work ahead of time as well as do a good job. These individuals' greatest dreams in life often involve wanting to leave their personal mark on the world. They would like to be remembered in some way, to have a lasting impression that signifies them. Thankfully, the number 22 in their chart makes the likelihood of this happening much greater. Most importantly, those with this number should always strive for modesty and humility, as they may tend to get too wrapped up in what they are good at and don't always stop to think that there may be someone better.

Expression Numbers One to 12

One

An individual with the number one is often very skilled in the world of business. They have a natural tact for entrepreneurship and often have grand ideas for new businesses they want to start. This individual will probably have many successful (and a few failed) businesses in their lifetime. They greatly enjoy being their own boss and many are known to find ways to live from home. Individuals with this number can also be very hypercritical of themselves or others. This can help create a quality business or organization, but if the individual does not keep this trait in check, they can push away those around them. People may find them overly judgmental or too harsh of a critic. Paying attention to this trait and learning to reign in their opinion will help maintain good, comfortable relationships with coworkers.

Two

Individuals with this number put a lot of weight on social prowess. They tend to be very skilled in the world of manners and elegance. These individuals usually have very high social skills and are very talented at marketing themselves and others. These people usually make brilliant marketing professionals and excel in the world of advertising. The hardest pill for this person to swallow is the fact that not everyone is going to like or get along with them. These individuals want to be friends with everyone and often cannot handle it when someone either clearly or secretly dislikes them. It would be beneficial for this person to remember that sometimes there is nothing you can do to make someone like you. These individuals may need to try and let it go if someone simply isn't getting along with them.

Three

Individuals with this number usually have increased skill in communication with others. Because of this, they tend to make brilliant writers, actors, and artists. They can often communicate feelings and emotions in a beautiful and elegant way that can be understood across a wide array of platforms and media. These individuals are often found in careers that involve some sort of self-expression because that is what they love to do. The flaw often found in these individuals is that they may have difficulty concentrating their thoughts into clear and concise information. They tend to go off on tangents and ramble for long periods. An individual with this number usually has to do a lot of editing to their writing and can often end up with mass amounts of cut material that has almost nothing to do with the end product. These individuals would benefit from thinking more clearly about what they are going to include in their projects and taking a moment to consider more deeply if it connects properly to what they are trying to convey.

Four

Individuals with this number often have skills in management and organization. They are often fair and impartial leaders who thrive in structure. These individuals are known for being reliable and consistent in their lives. These individuals tend to reject the unconventional and like to live in stable, structured environments. These people tend to find themselves in nine to five jobs where they have some sort of managerial status. Risk takers, these individuals are not. They are not likely to take jobs for companies that are up and coming or that appear to be rapidly growing or shrinking; they prefer to find employment within a well-established company. These individuals are faithful and loyal to those close to them. The biggest negative to this person is their tendency to focus too hard on the things that are outside their grasp. They tend to get caught up on the barriers that block them from things that they want and would benefit from focusing more on the things that are within their capabilities.

Five

These individuals are quite the separation from their neighbor, number four. These people live for adventure and love excitement. They practically ooze curiosity and are known to throw themselves into every new mini obsession they develop. They despise structured and organized careers and would rip their hair out in a typical nine to five job. These individuals crave freedom and constant stimulation.

These individuals' greatest talents are their ability to pick up random unusual skills seemingly out of the blue. By working hard, these individuals can learn how to do anything from fixing a car to juggling. Because of their charismatic and energetic demeanor (and their love of travel), these individuals often have a large group of friends from very different cultural and geographic backgrounds. Fives, unfortunately, tend to have a higher chance of becoming addicted to things like alcohol, drugs, and even sex. Their need to experience new and interesting things can often have consequences that they either don't notice or outright ignore at that moment.

Six

Individuals with this number are often very committed to speaking up for the underdog. They usually are the pushers of political movements and have a talent of getting others to agree with them purely through their conviction. These individuals are often known to be extremely passionate about the things that they are involved in. They are usually representatives or heads of nonprofits. From time to time, these individuals tend to put others before themselves too much. That is to say – they tend to push their needs and skills to the side to accommodate those which they believe to need help more. It would be beneficial to these individuals to remember that they are important as well and should focus more time and energy towards themselves.

Seven

These individuals are often very analytical and usually quite skilled at finding answers to complex questions. They usually make brilliant scientists or engineers. These people are usually very skilled at mathematics and science because they have a rare ability to see every detail and remember every last part of a process. These individuals are known for having a strong urge to seek the truth in everyday life. They are constantly asking questions about why things happen and are usually inclined to find the answer no matter what. These individuals are very determined to understand the world around them and often find that if they have not found the answers they seek, by a certain age, they may sink into a difficult depression. These individuals would benefit from remembering that some things in life are not meant to be understood.

Eight

Individuals with this number have only one goal in life: to win. These individuals are extremely competitive in almost everything that they do. They want to be number one in everything and are willing to fight hard for it. These are the type of people to turn everything into a competition, but they are also the type to work the absolute hardest for something they want. The greatest skill of this individual is their ability to focus on an end goal and push themselves past their current fatigue to reach that goal. These individuals care very little about their own comfort in a given situation. These individuals sometimes tend to work a little too hard and should remind themselves that it is often more important to take a break than to finish something.

Nine

Individuals with this number are often described as being philanthropic and a humanitarian. They are often very passionate about the activities they are involved in. These individuals are very powerful in their belief in themselves. These people often believe so strongly that they can accomplish anything that they usually do. It is these individuals' pure willpower that sets them apart from the crowd. They are often their own champions and have no trouble cheering themselves on their whole life. With this strong high can sometimes mean a strong low as well. This means that while these individuals believe very strongly that they can do anything, if they are not able to do something important to them, they may fall into a deep depressive state.

11

Individuals with this number can be annoying with just how many skills they have. These individuals possess the ability to maintain any of the skills present in any of the other numbers. They have a beautiful charisma and often a sort of magnetism that attracts others to them. These individuals are often known to have psychic or supernatural abilities and a stronger connection to the metaphysical than others. Because of the wide range of abilities and personality traits that this individual may have, they often have difficulty with an inner sense of contradiction. They may struggle with seeing themselves as hypocritical. Finding a balance amongst all of their skills and emotions would be beneficial for these individuals.

12

Individuals with this number often find themselves described as a visionary. This number is often considered representative of the "Master Builder", and as such, these individuals are often brilliant craftsmen. They may be woodworkers or contractors or even architects. All of these professions are areas that these individuals thrive in. Someone of this number is exceptionally skilled at creating things and bringing life to ideas. These individuals are often very motivating to be around and easily inspire those who experience them firsthand. These people are blessed with strong potential and are often considered "gifted" in their youth. In their youth, these individuals should begin concocting some of their grandest schemes and considering how to bring them into reality. While it may take many years before they can do so, the fleshing out of these ideas beforehand will typically give them a strong base to start with. These individuals can sometimes have difficulty accepting their failures. They want everything they build to be perfect and can't handle it when they are not.

Life Path Number One to 12

One

Individuals with this number often strive for excellence in everything that they do. They are true leaders and are very skilled at being kind and fair. These individuals are always sending themselves 'out there' with the intention of accomplishing something above and beyond normal measures. And these individuals usually do accomplish these things. These people are often at their best and the most motivated when staring in the face of adversity. They are often pushed to accomplish incredible things when everyone believes they will not. A person with this number will accomplish huge things in their life and will choose a life path that is difficult but motivating.

Two

Individuals with this number are often inclined to want and yearn for peace in their everyday life. Often getting coined under the term "Peacemaker", these individuals strive for just that – peace and love amongst people. They are often problem solvers who like to spend time coming up with solutions to common societal problems. These people often have great judgment; they make great court judges as they are known for being fair and kind. These individuals are often remembered in history as the heads of peaceful protests and known for coming up with calm solutions for issues.

Three

Those with this number are often brilliant public speakers. They often have great skills in communication and creating friends with those very different from them. They tend to live in the now and take challenges as they come. These individuals will often make choices based on how they are feeling in the moment rather than how they will feel in the future, and sometimes can suffer for it.

Four

Individuals with this number are often very skilled at seeing things through and bringing to life ideas in their head. These individuals are "Finishers"; they never do things that they do not see themselves committing to for the long haul. They are very dependable and can be trusted with big projects.

Five

These people are typically infatuated with diversity and are very adventurous. They love to learn and experience different cultures around the globe. These individuals typically lead a life full of excitement and adventure but lacking in organization.

Six

Individuals with this number are often known for being nurturing and caring. These individuals usually care very deeply in familial values. They often choose a life that allows them to be very involved in their families and may work from home or not work at all but choose to be a stay-at-home parent.

Seven

This number usually leans towards traits having to do with detail and analytics. Individuals are typically good accountants and are great at handling things involving money or numbers. They tend to choose lives that are structured and reliable.

Eight

Individuals with this number are very ambitious. They typically have very big goals that they work very hard to accomplish. They are strongest in the face of problems and are great at finding easy solutions to tough issues. These individuals typically choose lives that relate to politics in some way.

Nine

These individuals are often described as humanitarian. They are typically very empathetic and compassionate to those around them. These individuals are typically not interested in money or power but have a yearning to help people in their daily life. These individuals may choose lives in which they are strongly associated with non-profit organizations.

11

Individuals with this number are often very inspiring to those around them. These individuals often make brilliant public speakers and inspirational life coaches. Because of the presence of the Master Number, these individuals tend to be more inclined to have psychic abilities or be more connected to spiritual energies than others.

12/22

These individuals are often expected to do great things, and their lives are very dependent upon themselves. People around these people typically have high expectations for them, and depending on how these individuals choose to live their lives, they can either exceed those expectations or not meet them at all. They are typically known as a "wild card" in this section of Numerology, full of potential but not guaranteed to use it.

Heart's Desire Number One to 12

One

These individuals often have a strong drive for independence. Their heart typically pulls them towards free and unconstrained lives without suffocating structure or organization. This allows for a certain level of confidence that is rare and should be prized.

Two

Individuals with this number are often drawn towards peace. They typically desire peaceful solutions to societal issues and are often drawn towards professions that enforce peace as a core value.

Three

Individuals with this number are often drawn to methods of self-expression. They typically have a desire for those around them to know how they feel and are typically very skilled at getting their emotions across.

Four

These individuals often have an undying desire for their lives to maintain a sense of order and organization. People with this number often crave stability and structure in their day-to-day life.

Five

The inner desire of individuals with this number is to travel and experience. These people yearn for freedom and to experience every culture they can. These individuals are lovers of food and wine.

Six

These individuals have an extremely strong desire to care and nurture those around them. Nothing matters more to them than the safety and happiness of others. They are often driven to great lengths to care for those close to them.

Seven

The heart's desire of these individuals is to learn all that can be learned in a lifetime. They yearn for knowledge and understanding. They are often driven towards professions that are academic in nature.

Eight

These individuals often have a set idea of what it means to be successful. Their heart's desire is often to gain this success. Whether it be money, fame, or intellect, these individuals will stop at nothing to achieve their idea of a successful life.

Nine

The individuals with this number are often drawn to the idea of a "Utopia". They typically have a very defined definition of what they believe to be a perfect life or society and are very driven towards this idea of perfection.

11

The individual with this number is often known for being very in tune with the world around them. They are typically described as an "old soul". They seem to have lived much longer than they really have.

12/22

The only true desire of an individual with this number is to be remembered. They often strive to create a lasting impression on the people around them and usually have a dream to leave their mark on the world.

The Birth Date Number One to 31

One

The individual with this number is often known for being very autonomous. These individuals like to make things happen and start new trends.

Two

This number signifies balance, and as a result, individuals born on this day often crave stability and balance.

Three

A person born on the third day often needs constant stimulation to be happy. They are very creative and need to constantly be doing something new to keep their creativity properly functioning.

Four

People born on this day are often very responsible and care very deeply about how others perceive them. They tend to be very organized and like for things to go in their respective locations.

Five

This number has a very special meaning due to its connection to the five points of the pentagram, the five senses, and the five elements. Due to this connection, individuals with this birth day number are often more in tune with their environment than others.

Six

Individuals with this number care very deeply for justice and believe very strongly in fairness for all parties. They are angered by injustice and are known to stand up for those wronged.

Seven

Individuals under this number are often extremely meticulous. They love detail and pay attention to every small part of a situation.

Eight

Eights are ambitious individuals. They have lots of stamina and are willing to work harder than anyone else to reach their goals.

Nine

Nines tend to be idealistic. They have a particular image of happiness and don't settle for less than that. They are very sacrificial and want everyone to be happy.

Ten

The tenth day is greatly significant in the world of divination. Individuals born on this day often have a desire to be the best at everything they do.

11

As a Master Number, this date is extremely potent. The power of this number lies in the potential for balance. This number represents two opposing forces that, when combined in harmony, can do great things.

12

This individual has all of the creative skill of the number three with the added organizational skills of number two and can create abstract art that still gives a clear and concise message.

13

These individuals are extremely analytic about themselves. Sometimes considered narcissistic, they often know themselves better than anyone else.

14

This number allows for extreme self-discipline. These individuals often take leaps of faith but think through these leaps carefully.

15

These individuals often have an affinity for yoga or meditation as their independent streak from the number one combines with their connection from the number five.

16

These individuals often have difficulty allowing others to make decisions and may be accused of having a superiority complex.

17

These individuals may have difficulty letting other people into their inner circle and find they would be much happier if they let others into their lives.

18

These individuals are very passionate about seemingly random things. They are often the type of people to start a clique movement and spearhead charities for rare diseases.

19

These individuals are extremely social and love to have big circles of friends around them at all times. They still possess a sort of independence courtesy of the number one but prefer to experience this independence with others.

20

These individuals often put their heart before their brain and may find themselves falling in love far too quickly. They often have a desire to be wanted or accepted and will do anything to keep the peace.

21

These individuals love working on crafts that use their hands or extenuate their sense of touch. This would include things like knitting, sewing, or building.

22

These individuals may have issues maintaining a constant in their life. They often drive for change, and as a result, may have many jobs before they are middle-aged. Despite this, they typically find themselves successful in life's endeavors.

23

These individuals are often searching for ways to be even more in tune with their environment than they already are. This can lead them to lives that are more naturalistic than normal. Think zero waste or minimalist lifestyles.

24

These individuals often have difficulty focusing on their work as they are distracted by others. They are extremely empathetic and cannot stop thinking about another's problems until they are "fixed".

25

These individuals tend to be obsessive-compulsive and have perfectionistic qualities. The work these people do is typically incredible, but they are almost never happy with it.

26

This individual usually has incredible personal accomplishment. Those accomplishments often have a way of pulling other people into success as well.

27

These individuals are very passionate but also contain a sort of realism that allows them to think clearly about their passions and put them into motion in an organized fashion.

28

These individuals need a partner in their life. They desire to be able to share their life with another and are often known to marry young and keep that relationship for longer than people would expect.

29

These individuals combine an idealistic and analytic tendency to create someone that can pay attention to every last detail, even in things that are abstract or don't seem to matter to the common onlooker.

30

These individuals are typically very accomplished and want more than anything to be appreciated for this accomplishment. They don't particularly care about how their accomplishment helps others.

31

These individuals are often extremely entrepreneurial as they possess many rare skills and can implement them without much thought. These skills are typically surprising and lead to great success.

How Numerology Can Affect Our Everyday

Numerology presents itself in interesting ways on a daily basis. The following is just one way that someone's Numerology may be the reason for incredible experiences.

Business

Erika has many ideas for new and groundbreaking businesses. Many of these are things that have never been done before and would be extremely successful, but she is having difficulty getting them off the ground. She tends not to think things through and cannot always tell if the marketplace is in a position to accept her ideas. Thankfully, she just had a breakthrough using her wide array of communication skills. She spoke to an already well-established business, and they agreed to sponsor her for her first few months of production. If not for her incredible persuasion skills, this never would have happened. Erika has a Personality Number of one, which gave her the 'never before seen' ideas. She has an Expression Number of one as well, which gives her the business ability to persuade the other business professionals. She has a Life Path Number of three, which gave her the communicational skills to convey her plan properly. She has the Heart's Desire Number of eight, which gave her the motivation and drive to run towards what she would view as her success. Finally, she has the Birth Date Number of 18, which allowed her to tap into untouched areas and come up with ideas that had not been fleshed out before.

Chapter 10: Kundalini Rising – What Is It?

Kundalini Rising (a.k.a. Kundalini Awakening) is based on the idea that all humans contain some sort of energy within the base of their spine called "Kundalini". The idea is that through vigorous meditation and yoga, this energy can be "Awakened" and thus travel up and down the spine through the body. This energy is often represented as a coiled snake at the base of the spine, which matches with its name which roughly translates into "coiled". The results of this awakening are said to cause states of extreme bliss and enlightenment. To reach this period, it is said that the Kundalini needs to pass through several chakra points inside the human body and along the spine. It is believed that once this energy is awakened, it does not ever return to its coiled state but will ebb and flow throughout the lifetime of that individual.

Kundalini in History

The roots of the Kundalini idea trace their way back to Ancient India, in the Indus Valley, Ancient Egypt, and Sumerian civilizations. Most notably we can see this in the Ancient Vedic texts in which numerous Rig-Veda hymns praise a liquid known as "Soma" that many believe to be a metaphor for this energy within us all. Kundalini has strong ties with the ancient god known as Lord Shiva, for Lord Shiva is always seen with a serpent wrapped around his neck which some argue represents Kundalini. Possibly the most notable allegorical record of Kundalini is an ancient Ramayana tale which tells the tale of a noble and his beautiful wife. In this tale, the noble, who goes by the name Rama, and his wife, who goes by the name Sita, are caught in escort with an evil demon called Ravana. Ravana kidnaps Sita, who is meant to encapsulate the ideal woman and perfect femininity, and imprisons her in an island fortress called "Lanka". It is well known within this tale that Lanka is meant to represent a physical human body and Sita is meant to represent the Kundalini energy. Ravana, on the other hand, is meant to represent the five senses and the five organs of action which are believed to lead man towards desire and away from their spirituality. He represents this symbolically with his ten heads. Rama is meant to represent the consciousness, and through powerful expertise, "releases" Sita, a very clear metaphor for the releasing of Kundalini within a human.

Kundalini Yoga

Yoga, in recent years, has come to the forefront of modern physical fitness. With its image as the skinny girl who can do the splits and balance perfectly with her leg over her head, it has become a very popular form of physical workout. While Kundalini Yoga does offer some form of physical exertion, it has a taste of spirituality to go along with it. Kundalini Yoga is often performed with a more worship-like air about it. Often taking place in almost complete silence and rarely in a gym, this workout is definitely different from many others. One of these differences is its vast spiritual history. This yoga is old and has managed to stay with almost the same principles for centuries. This is partially due to the fact that Kundalini does not have any overwhelming strict or suffocating dogmas to steer away practitioners. Kundalini allows itself not to be a strict religion but simply to be a tool one can use to find their inner spirituality. In ancient times, yoga was not confined by the definition of physical activity but, in fact, was considered simply a connection to one's spiritual self through their bodies. They had no goals of physical fitness but rather a connection to the energy they believe lives within us all – and for this connection, they stressed the fact that no buffer was necessary. No prayer or food or special dance – simply to practice and focus. In fact, it is recorded that the first Kundalini sessions consisted of almost entirely no physical activity whatsoever. Disciples simply sat in front of their master and listened to their revelations about spirit. This practice was very common in Ancient Vedic times and was later replicated in religious figures known as Buddha and Jesus. Throughout the years, this method of spirituality evolved until it began to include the physical acting out of the spiritual visions. This then evolved into what we know as yoga today. One of the reasons that this form of spiritual expression is not commonly known or spoken of today is due to its secretiveness throughout history. For thousands of years, the study of Kundalini was kept secret and sacred, known only by an inner group of spiritualists and their students. This was often explained through the idea that the public was not ready or prepared for such incredible knowledge and that the awakening of Kundalini amongst the average folk would cause chaos and destruction. Kundalini would still be mostly lost to western society if not for the teachings of a man known as "Yogi Bahjan". Yogi chose to impart his wisdom upon the youth of the United States due to the uprising of the hippie movement in the late 1960s. He came to America and found hundreds of youth desperately wanting to be closer to their spiritual side and going about it in all the wrong ways through drugs and mysticism. He taught over 8,000 yoga classes and also released a handful of books on the subject. At the beginning of his career, he is also credited with establishing the Healthy, Happy, Holy Organization. Without this man, Kundalini Yoga and subsequent Awakening would never have reached the States.

Chapter 11: Kundalini Rising and You

Now that you fully understand the origins of Kundalini and how it has reached us, it is time to learn how you too can awaken the energy within. With the internet today, anyone can find hundreds and hundreds of ways to awaken the energy within them. However, the average person must approach these with caution, as this energy is extremely powerful, and without the learned expertise, over time they may harm themselves or their chakra balances.

Warning: we highly recommend that the reader consults with an expert regarding the awakening of their energy for their life before attempting to do so.

> 1) The first step to awakening your chakra energy is to practice mindful breathing exercises. To begin, you will want to relax and take several cleansing breaths in and out. You will want to begin to practice a sort of soft abdominal breathing – these are soft, calm breaths within you that eventually bring your abdomen and lungs to an equilibrium of gases.

2) Now, you will want to find with your mind's eye (this is easiest done with your eyes closed) the location of your kidneys. This may sound strange, but you simply have to visualize it in the lower back of your body are your two kidneys. Visualize them and imagine their location.

3) You will want to "massage" the kidneys by releasing several breaths of air that expel all the air from your lungs and the bag within your abdomen.

4) At this point, to help with your breathing, you will want to begin chanting the phrase "Num Mum Yum Pa'Hum." As you exhale, you will want to focus and try to feel for the vibration of the right Adrenal, the Right Kidney and then the subsequent left Adrenal or Left Kidney.

5) If you are having difficulty feeling the vibration in your kidneys, you can rub your lower back to promote the activity.

6) You will now want to make sure that you are in a comfortable position.

7) You will physically want to lift your arms above your head with your thumbs out. You will want to make sure your shoulders are rotated down and back. Rotating your thumbs back and forth, you should be able to feel the connection of your thumbs to your lungs.

8) You will now want to reach your index finger towards the sky and feel the large intestine connect to the ribcage.

9) You will want to lift your collarbones and feel a responding suspension of the kidneys.

10) Think back with your mind's eye to the airbags and their connection to the kidneys.

11) You will now want to tuck the chin and release a small bit of air from the diaphragm.

12) Inhale deeply, feel the air bags, and make sure that the chin, tongue, palate, and sinuses are stacked neatly with a connection to the spinal cord.

13) Exhale slowly. You should feel the top of your lungs buoy upwards.

14) Inhale again touching the top of the chest and bottom of the abdomen.
15) Exhale and feel the chakra point at the top of the nose.
16) Breathe again, letting the chakra point expand.
17) Feel the vertebrae of your spinal cord lift and extend upwards slightly.

Practicing this meditation system on a regular basis can help guide you to your own Kundalini Awakening.

Now we will describe some of the common side effects and positive as well as negative experiences of those who have awakened their own energy within themselves. Kundalini energy is often described as a sensation of electricity or internal lightning bolts within the person at the sight of the awakening. People are often described to shake or jerk their body parts or limbs. This is usually completely out of the control of the individual who is awakening their energy. You may also feel upon the awakening of this energy a sensation of insects crawling along your spinal cord, along with feelings of either intense heat or intense cold. The individual in question may also feel an intense moment of pleasure that sometimes leads to an orgasmic state. They also may experience sudden and unexplainable mood swings, far beyond normal highs and lows. As a result of this awakening, people often report having much more empathetic bonds with those around them. They have also said that this increased level of empathy results in telepathic or psychic abilities. Aging has been said to slow as a result of the rising of Kundalini as well as the increase in creative ability and charismatic personality traits. These individuals often say that the great mysteries of life are no longer mysteries; they are connected more deeply to all that is and ever was.

An individual in search of the enlightenment that comes with the awakening of Kundalini is strongly urged to consult with professionals and support groups on the matter. Trying to find an experienced Kundalini yoga instructor who has experienced an awakening themselves will greatly help someone who's desire it is to awaken this incredible power. Attempting to awaken this power on your own can result in terrible consequences as well as simply not working at all. Many support groups can be found online, and Kundalini Yoga instructors are common in larger cities. If you have trouble finding one in your local area, many online instructors openly give their knowledge to the public. They can be found on YouTube, Pinterest, and blog sites. Many YouTube videos have been made on the process of awakening the Kundalini as well as how to cope with the aftermath. If you have experienced an awakening or would like to, we would highly recommend searching through these.

Conclusion

From the origins of humanity's biggest questions to the modern-day awakening of deep and ancient energy that lies within us all, this text has covered a significant amount of ancient divinity. We will sum up this text within these next few sentences by going over the topics we have touched on since the beginning of this book.

In Chapter 1, we introduced horoscopes and gave some background on their origins and how they have begun to rise in popularity to become the commonality we see in mainstream media today. In Chapter 2, we went through the common stereotypes of each Zodiac sign and explained why a lot of them are based on fact but not wholly the truth. We went in-depth into the common traits associated with each Zodiac sun sign as well as how they work in real-life scenarios. In Chapter 3, we delved into the depths of someone's birth chart. We began by explaining the importance of each house of the chart and how they relate to each other. We spoke of each of the planets that house the Zodiac as well as the Transcendental planets, which are those that are not found in traditional Astrology. Finally, we gave an example birth chart to help the reader understand the dynamics of reading and interpreting the birth chart. Chapter 4 we devoted entirely to the Ascendant, which is a section of the birth chart that often goes unnoticed but that holds arguably more power within your birth chart than your sun sign. In Chapter 5, we gave a more in-depth history of Tarot cards and the common uses of them in history. Chapter 6 began the discussion about Tarot cards and their extensive background. We attempted to cover as much about Tarot cards as possible and still only managed to scratch the surface. We went in-depth into the meaning of each of the cards found in the Major Arcana series, which is often seen as the core of the Tarot deck. In Chapter 7, we connected all of the previous ideas covered and gave examples of how all of the different forms of divinity work together to create one whole rather than one section being completely in charge of an individual's personality and life choices. The next chapter, Chapter 8, began to delve into Numerology. We began by explaining how an average person can calculate the various Numerology numbers found within their names and birthdates. We then gave an in-depth meaning behind each of the numbers that we calculated. Finally, we finished this chapter by giving real-life examples of how these numbers can present themselves in a person's everyday life. In Chapter 10, we gave a deeper history of Kundalini Rising and its significance in the hippy movement. We also gave some examples of its presence in ancient texts and stories. We also gave a quick rundown on how the Kundalini Yoga organization came to America in the 1960s. Finally, in the last chapter, Chapter 11, we gave a quick and shortened guide for awakening the Kundalini through meditation and yoga. We then gave some of the common side effects to awakening this energy within you.

Throughout this text, we have given many examples of how each of these forms of divinity can affect an individual within their daily lives. Now that we have reached the ending of this text, we would like to express how important it is to consider every different type of divinity when attempting to understand your inner self better. No one method of understanding gives the entire picture, as humans are incredibly and wildly complicated in every aspect of their lives. Simply looking at the sun sign or just your Personality Number will not give the reader the understanding they are looking for. If they truly wish to understand why they think a certain way or why certain things befall them, it is within their best interest to consider every side to their own story. You are simply not doing yourself justice by only looking at one tiny aspect of divination. You will find that many of your actions and decisions make much more sense when you look at it all together – each part making up a small aspect of your true being. Within this text, we were not able to cover every single bit of information that would be required to understand yourself truly. If you would like to reach this true understanding, we would highly recommend that the reader continue to read separate books on subjects such as Astrology, Numerology, and Tarot. Moreover, if you happen to be interested in the subject of Kundalini Awakening and would like to unlock the incredible power of this intense energy, it would be within your best interest to continue to research the internet and other e-books of this sort.

Part 2: Tarot

An Essential Beginner's Guide to Psychic Tarot Reading, Tarot Card Meanings, Tarot Spreads, Numerology, and Astrology

Introduction

Have you always been interested in tarot, but you just didn't know where to start? Have you wondered if you were psychic and had no way to test it out? Have you had a tarot deck sitting on your shelf for ages that you haven't touched because you weren't sure? If you've answered "yes" to any of these questions, this book is the one for you!

Welcome to *Tarot: An Essential Beginner's Guide to Psychic Tarot Reading, Tarot Card Meanings, Tarot Spreads, Numerology, and Astrology*. Welcome, and congratulations for downloading this book. You will not regret doing so, for the following pages are full of information you can use to not only understand the tarot (finally!) but to literally change your life.

The book will begin with an examination of the history of tarot cards and their usage across time in Chapter 1 before going into the art of the tarot itself in Chapter 2. In that second chapter, you'll learn about how to connect with your intuition, how to choose a deck, and what the pros and cons of tarot happen to be.

Chapter 3 introduces you to all 78 cards in the tarot deck before providing some tips and tricks for memorization. Chapter 4 reveals 20 different spreads you can use for your own tarot readings, and

Chapter 5 provides 10 exercises and brain boosters for your practice (as well as 3 overall tips for the tarot trade).

Chapter 6 demonstrates how tarot is intimately connected with numerology and astrology; then Chapter 7 discloses a method you can use to make tarot a part of your career in the future. By the end of this book, you should feel that you've received all the information you need to be able to read tarot cards for yourself and others. You should feel confidently psychic and ready to take on the world!

While there are several books about tarot on the market today, your choice to download this one deserves my eternal gratitude. Thank you from the bottom of my heart! I hope *Tarot: An Essential Beginner's Guide* gives you all that you wished for and more. Enjoy the experience and remember to keep your heart and mind open to everything tarot wants to teach you!

Chapter 1: Tarot History

Tarot is essentially a card game designed to tell fortunes and reveal the future. It didn't start off that way, though! At first, tarot was simply a deck of cards for playing card games socially. At first, tarot decks were only comprised of those original 56 cards, and they hardly looked anything like they do today.

In the early days of tarot, the deck was rather simple. With no Major Arcana section whatsoever, there were just the court/face cards and the remaining 40 suited cards, with each suit counting ace-10. The early days of tarot were also likely not as ancient as you'd like to think. Early days of tarot were simply the late 14th and early 15th centuries.

Tarot Practices Across Time

While many ancient cultures surely had their own means of divination, it is unlikely that the actual tarot deck of today existed anywhere across time except from around the turn of the 15th century. There is no archaeological proof of this long-time connection, and we have virtually no historical proof of the tarot's existence unless we look at Europe around the 15th century.

Despite this concrete history – which places the first tarot decks being released and played (casually, as a card game; not as a divination tool) around 1375 – it is possible that the ancient mysteries and archetypes revealed by the Major Arcana cards especially – which weren't added to the deck until around 1450 – may have actually been passed down from ancient cultures across the world.

The symbols in the tarot seem older than time itself. Perhaps this is why people freely speculate about tarot being older than history can prove. Perhaps this is why people across the world can relate to the cards. The symbols speak to us in ways we often can't put words to, and that's the essence of divination. Interestingly enough, however, these images on both the Major *and* Minor Arcana cards were added to the deck much later.

I already explained how the Major Arcana section of the deck came later, around 1450, as opposed to when the tarot was "invented," around 1350. However, it is useful to explain this history a little more. Tarot was originally played as a parlor game called Triumph that was similar to Bridge today, and that game had absolutely no divination intent. However, with growing interest in divination in Europe around the turn of the 17th century, people began to associate their own, much deeper meanings to the cards.

At this time, the deck would have consisted of a detailed Major Arcana section with a far simpler Minor Arcana section, and the court/face cards may have been beautiful, but the pip cards (numbering ace-10) would have been extremely simple with just the cups, swords, wands, and coins – nothing else. Even around the turn of the 19th century, the deck was still incredibly simple, without much adornment on those pip cards, but people were *much* more fascinated in the tarot as a means of divination than anything else at this time.

In fact, the first divination-only tarot deck was designed and released on the European market by Jean-Baptiste Alliette in 1791. This French occultist developed the imagery on the Major Arcana and court/face cards extensively, but the pip cards were still largely neglected. It wasn't until the turn of the 20th century that a follower of Aleister Crowley's philosophy, Arthur Waite, teamed up with fellow occultist and artist Pamela Colman Smith in order to design the cards as we know them today. At this point, tarot got its first distinctly American influences, and the study of tarot increased in popularity, allowing it to spread across the world like wildfire.

Waite insisted on the importance of including people and imagery on the pip cards as well as all the others, if not for any other reason than to give the card readers at home a little more to work with on those previously basic cards. Smith's artwork was finalized, and the deck was released to the world under the name of the Rider-Waite deck, although some still call it the Waite-Smith deck in recognition of the artist herself.

Debate Over Origins

There are legends about the first tarot deck originating in Ancient Egypt. Popular theories from the late 18th century tend to support this claim, but there's not much actual history behind this connection. It was in 1781 that a Frenchman named Antoine Court de Gebelin claimed this ancient Egyptian connection through a paper he had published. He was convinced that the images on the Major Arcana cards were taken directly from the mythology and cosmology of Ancient Egypt. He even claimed that the Catholic Church and the popes knew of this age-old connection and that they wanted desperately to keep it hidden. Of course, people at the time loved this story, and despite its lack of historical background, they bought it hook, line, and sinker.

There are legends that the tarot deck originated in Gypsy culture. People see the mystical images on the cards and associate them with the eccentricity and occultism they stereotypically expect from gypsies across time. Popular culture hasn't helped with these stereotypes either. There are frequent depictions in films of gypsies with tarot decks or of them simply reading peoples' fortunes. And while gypsies surely had their own nomadic/indigenous styles of earth magic and divination, if they *were* associated with tarot decks, it was probably because someone picked up a deck of parlor playing cards and then infused it with his or her own meaning. Tarot wouldn't have been all that accessible to gypsies otherwise unless someone was able to make his or her own deck from scratch.

There are legends that the tarot deck originated from Kabbalistic Jewish practice. The Major Arcana's symbols match the same number as paths to follow in the Kabbalah's Tree of Life. There are 22 of each, and the symbols align almost perfectly. People love to speculate that the imagery and symbolism were meant to be aligned because these cards were first designed by these people, but that historical hunch is incredibly hard to prove. It's much more likely that the rise of occultist interest around the turn of the 20th century in Europe influenced tarot deck artists (and therefore, the way the cards looked) to create decks that *appeared* as if more Kabbalistic secrets had been infused all along. Surely, around this time, Hermetic Mysticism crept into the deck as well, and Egyptian symbolism, mythology, and cosmology have already been infused into the deck almost a century before.

There are even legends that the tarot deck originated around the (decidedly less ancient) time of the Cathars, circa 1150. The Cathars were a practicing sect of Christianity that believed Roman Catholicism worshipped idols and held impure beliefs about their own power. They practiced a much more orthodox sect of Christianity, but it was also somehow more aligned with what we today see as the "occult." These Cathars believed in reincarnation, practicing rituals, and the ancient mysteries of this Earth. Some people, therefore, think that Cathars may have produced the first images for the Major Arcana cards (although, in reality, those cards weren't produced until around three centuries later).

Tarot decks are not as pure and ancient as we once thought. It turns out they've been altered and adapted greatly over time, too, which is perhaps a part of why their exact origin feels so difficult to pinpoint. Additionally, the tarot's images are poignant, and their symbolistic meanings feel ubiquitous, reaching across language and cultural barriers to express truths about humanity as a whole. Tarot certainly feels ancient. I would have believed that tarot arose out of Ancient Egypt if someone I trusted insisted on it, but that's why doing your own research can be so important and validating.

The history of tarot proves that tracking down the deck's exact origins is complicated, an enfolding process like trying to escape from a maze. The more you think you know, the more there is to correct your thinking. Regardless of where and when the tarot arose, however, it's here for us today, and its abilities to help us are extensive. There are so many possibilities to do with the spread or layouts of cards. You can get so many different kinds of decks these days. You can take classes to learn more about tarot, both online and in person. You can download apps on your devices devoted to tarot so you can learn on the go. It almost doesn't matter where tarot came from because it's clearly a constant work in progress that keeps getting strengthened, enhanced, and adapted through time. As you can, just be grateful that it's here for you today, relax and feel supported by this knowledge, grab a nearby deck of tarot cards, and let them connect you with your fate.

Chapter 2: The Art of Tarot

Regardless of how old it is exactly, tarot is a divinatory art that uses symbols, numbers, and connections to the collective unconscious in order to express its meaning. It's designed like a card game with 78 cards, versus the standard deck with 52 cards. It's not played like a standard deck of cards, either. Tarot relies on ancient mysteries to establish its visual truth, and by arranging the cards in a certain fashion, you can receive insight into your issues or illnesses, and you can obtain messages from your higher self and the universe.

Connecting to Intuition

Tarot card reading is so much more about connecting to one's higher self than it is about divining the inherent truth of the cards. The cards always contain the same images and the same basic meanings, but by *your* shuffling and intentional questioning of the deck, the cards group into arrangements that reveal deep and lasting truths that will resonate only for the querent. However, it must be emphasized that the cards are not the entities that hold power with tarot, and neither is the querent (the person you're drawing cards *for* or *about*). The *reader* of the cards is that entity, and his or her higher self is the center of that power.

When you decide that you're ready to embrace tarot and start reading the cards, remember this truth as you proceed. It doesn't necessarily matter what deck you choose, for it's much more important *how* you use the cards of any deck. Use the deck for healing and growth purposes, and it will never do anyone harm. There are certainly rumors that tarot is evil, unholy, or that it invites in spirits that can hurt you. I say now, firmly, tarot isn't about that. Tarot is simply about the reader of the cards connecting with his or her higher self in an effort to answer questions and to heal.

When you engage in your own readings of the cards, remember the importance of your intuition, for it is your direct channel to your higher self. If you ever feel that something I've written doesn't jive with your intuition, please don't force yourself to accept it! Your intuition is your highest truth, and it is much more valuable to you than my words are. If indeed you *do* have this experience with any guidance or associations I elucidate, make a note in your own tarot journal or the pages of this book (if you've chosen to print it). Keep record of these insights, for they are so endlessly helpful for you, both now and in the future.

Choosing Your Deck

Choosing your deck is one of the most fun (although sometimes stressful) moments for the beginning practitioner of tarot. There is certainly a number to choose from. If you're looking at decks online, there are probably *hundreds* of options. If you're looking at your local bookstore or metaphysical store, there are still a lot, but hopefully not quite so many. As you go about making these choices, follow the guidelines below for some assistance.

How to Apply Intuition

Remember that your intuition is your inherent connection with your higher self. As you strive to choose a tarot deck for yourself, it's so essential that you learn to let your intuition be your guide. Whether you're shopping online or in person, try this exercise to apply your intuition to the task:

> Gather 3-4 potential tarot decks that you really like. Hold the options in-hand (or in your real or virtual shopping cart). Sit with these options for a while and try to turn off your thinking mind. Almost enter a meditative state as you take in your options and reject any logic-based choices. You want the choice to arise totally naturally as if it's been your truth all along.

Psychic Choices

If you're having trouble using your intuition, you can go a step further to see what your psychic choice would be. It might seem counter-intuitive that making a psychic choice would be easier than making an intuitive choice, but the trick in this instance is your eyes. When you're working through intuition, you'll want to keep your eyes open so that you're using some part of your mind to make the selection. It's important that you struggle through what's logical versus what's deeper, truer, and emotional.

When you're working through psychic potential, however, you'll want those eyes 100% shut. Close off your physical body to any influences whatsoever, and let your psychic powers guide your choice. Again, this method works for both in-store and online shopping. For online shoppers, gather all the potential items in your "shopping cart," close your eyes, spin around a few times if you can, and then point out the deck that's meant to be yours. Open your eyes at the very end to see which one you selected.

Types of Decks

There are so many different kinds of decks that it's almost overwhelming to approach. For your ease, it will help to know that some decks are specifically tarot decks while some will say they are "Oracle Decks." These Oracle decks are totally different. While the tarot has 78 cards, divided between 22 Major Arcana and 56 Minor Arcana, Oracle decks can have any number of cards, and each one is like its own Major Arcana card with impressive themes and meanings. Additionally, there are no court/face cards, and no numbered "pip" cards (like the 4 of Wands, 8 of Cups, etc.) in an Oracle deck. Overall, I'd steer clear of Oracle decks if you truly want to work with tarot (although Oracle decks are equally awesome and fun in their own right).

Another tip is that some tarot decks are oriented toward themes that may not resonate with you. There are black cat tarot decks, Egyptian-themed tarot decks, gay culture tarot decks, "Animal Wisdom" tarot decks, David Bowie-themed tarot decks, unicorn tarot decks, medieval-themed tarot decks, renaissance-themed tarot decks, wartime tarot decks, "Wild Unknown" tarot decks, "Tarot Apokalypsis" decks, Age of Aquarius tarot decks, Druid-themed tarot decks, animals & nature tarot decks, Illuminati tarot decks, and so much more. Finally, there are the basic decks that use the same essential imagery from the Rider-Waite tarot deck with just a unique flourish from the artist. (The Rider-Waite tarot deck was designed and released in 1909 and is the most basic, most traditional deck still produced in mass today).

Furthermore, there are decks with large-sized cards versus small-sized cards, and I always recommend that bigger cards are better (especially for starting practitioners!). There are also decks that come with their own explanatory books, while there are decks that come alone. I prefer the ones with the attached books – I can never get enough tarot books, though!

much later

Pros & Cons

Generally, follow these pros & cons as you decide which deck will be yours.

Pros:

- Large card size
- Relatable theme
- No discernable theme
- Package comes with a detailed book
- Definitely a tarot deck (not an Oracle deck)
- Relatable art
  - <u>A note on this point</u>: Some tarot decks only show white people, and that won't matter for some, but it will absolutely ostracize other practitioners. The reader of the cards must be able to relate to the art on the cards, so seek out art that reflects your skin color if you can. Again, this note is more helpful for some than others, for I know that some people won't be bothered by this element whatsoever.
- The deck seemingly chose you
- Good paper quality
- Attached book is large, extensive, detailed, and well-written
- Good reviews of the product (for online shoppers)
- Good card thickness
- Perfectly affordable within your means

Cons:

- Cards are too small
- Not a relatable theme for you
- Theme is too "loud" in the cards / is distracting
- No book comes with the package
- It's an Oracle deck, not a tarot deck
- Not relatable art
- Someone chose the deck for you / you don't think it chose you
- Poor paper quality
- Attached book is small or poorly-written

- Poor reviews of the product (for online shoppers)
- Cards feel too thick or too thin
- Not affordable within your current means

Reading the Cards

Now that you've received some assistance in choosing your deck, you're going to need to understand exactly what you're getting yourself into. Tarot is a beautiful divination art that allows you to connect with realms deep within and far outside the self. It's a helpful tool used to provide growth, balance, support, and flourishing to anyone's life. There are so many different things you can do with a tarot deck, too. It might all look the same for you're always just shuffling cards and drawing some out of the deck, but the *intention* behind these acts can vary significantly to the potential benefit of so many people.

Decision Making

Tarot is an excellent tool to boost one's decision-making abilities. So many people these days are indecisive or unsure how to resolve large issues that loom over their lives. So many people, too, are hoping for growth but don't know the right direction. Tarot can provide that decision, resolution, growth, direction, and more, with hardly anything done on the individual's part aside from placing one's hands on the deck and asking a question to the universe. Tarot can help you make the tough choices that you face, and truly enables anyone to regain control over his or her life from here on out. From now on, with the assistance of tarot, you'll be able to:

- Choose your life path with confidence;
- Learn how to own up to your mistakes;
- Uncover the reasons behind your anxieties, fears, and diseases;
- Make simple decisions easier through 1- to 5-card pulls;

- Discern your motivation;
- Assess most likely outcomes;
- Assert your values and ideal situations;
- and so much more.

Quality of Life

Tarot can remind you that you are in control of your life. It often feels like we're being thrown through situations and experiences like a rag doll, but we as humans have an incredible amount of free will! When you ask questions of the tarot, the answers provided come from the reader's higher self, and they are almost always inflected with divine intention. Therefore, these answers are not going to direct you toward failure or floundering or loss. They're only going to urge you toward growth, but it's up to *you* to choose whether or not you follow the path revealed to you by the cards. Look forward to the following benefits to your life after working with tarot:

- Enhanced compassion and empathy for others;
- Amplified ability to empower yourself and others;
- Developed, honed, and focused psychic abilities;
- Increased potential for creativity and creative expression;
- Enhanced self-awareness and consciousness of the world;
- Increased trust in your intuition and higher self;
- Better understanding of how much will power one has;
- and so much more.

Insight & Life Help

Tarot can also generally provide insight into one's circumstances and assist anyone in need (whether they're in need of direction, assistance, clarity, or otherwise). Tarot spreads are perfectly designed for this task, and you will find 20 detailed spreads to choose from in Chapter 4. Furthermore, by connecting the reader with his or her intuition, psychic abilities, and higher self, that person will be aided deeply. Additionally, both readers and querents will experience increased and enhanced abilities to heal and receive guidance from the universe. Ask the cards one short question or a long, detailed one. You're sure to receive helpful insights and tidbits for refreshed direction in the future.

Helping Others & World Healing

As you master the tarot, you'll be increasingly knowledgeable, empathetic, and willing to help others. You'll find your capacity for patience boosted, and as a reader of the cards, you'll carry great responsibility to share this patience and fresh knowledge with others. With this knowledge, you'll also carry information about the greatest archetypal energies known to humankind across time. You will carry the stories, you will bear the burdens, but you will also hold the key that unchains all our shackles. As you grow in your knowledge and appreciation of tarot, don't be afraid to ask questions that will benefit individuals, whole groups of people, or the Earth as a planet and nurturing entity. Widen your scope, open your eyes, and proceed bravely without fear. With knowledge comes great responsibility, but don't worry – I guarantee you'll love every minute of it.

Chapter 3: The Cards

The most essential part of understanding the tarot is being able to access the meanings of the cards themselves. What does the Emperor mean? What is the suit of Cups all about? What's a Page of Swords? What's an Ace mean in this deck? What if I pull a card that's upside-down? All these questions and more will be answered in this chapter, and you will end this section feeling confident that there's a substantial well of knowledge to draw from when you conduct your first tarot readings.

Major Arcana

The Major Arcana, also called the Greater Arcana, reveals the inner mysteries of humanity. They tell the story of humanity in the form of 22 archetypal images, and each piece of the story reveals deep truths about the nature of existence as a human in this reality. The 22 cards in the Major Arcana are numbered from 0-21 or 1-22. Occasionally, the Major Arcana starts with 0 (the Fool), but I've listed the Fool last here, as number 22, which is equally common. The point with the Fool is that it begins the cycle and when that cycle ends, the Fool starts it up again; therefore, it exists on both extremes and earns its right to be both 0 and 22.

Some decks will have a "Major Arcana" section with numbered cards 1-22 without these same card names. Worry not – the archetypes are still always the same in deeper meaning. Even with different names, card 1 from the Major Arcana will always represent what the Magician does; card 2 will always relate to the High Priestess's energy, card 3 will always signify the Empress's energy, and so on.

For your convenience, in this chapter, I've explained what each card means when it's right-side-up as well as when it's upside-down. When you pull a card upside-down, it's called "in reverse," and it typically lessens the effect of the card in question, but occasionally, it means that matters will be more intense than what the card describes.

1. The Magician. The Magician is all about seeing your path ahead, making decisions, and taking actions. This card signifies that it's time to follow your dreams. There has been time for introspection, but now is the time for action. The Magician represents a powerful source of inspiration that is ready to act as your muse, and it predicts that you will be able to work on complex projects at this time. This card stands for finding your flow, taking first steps, becoming empowered, embracing your will power, activating your energy, following direction, and engaging in creativity. Power and success lie ahead.

In reverse, the Magician signifies that your flow has become blocked. There are projects you dream of that just aren't working out. It might not be your fault, so look at the cards that appear around the Magician in reverse to find clues to this issue.

2. The High Priestess. The High Priestess card is all about appreciating the feminine in the world. This card suggests the value of stillness, contemplation, passivity, sensitivity, reflection, and depth. This card tells you that you can manifest your dreams as long as you're open to the mysterious feminine energy within you. Overall, the High Priestess stands for the divine feminine, initiation, gateways, the collective unconscious, true wisdom, dream guidance, and powerful intuition. In reverse, the High Priestess signifies that you'll need to take a step back in life in order to access this divine feminine grace and insight. You might need to tone things down, or you may be caught up in delusions that distract you from this capacity. It's time to find stillness and refocus so that things don't turn disastrous.

3. The Empress. The Empress card suggests that abundance is headed your way. This card represents the potential of abundance through reproduction as well as financial prosperity in your life and more. For those invested in the reproductive meaning, this card signifies fertility, creation, and the product of two true lovers. For those divested from this meaning, this card is still incredibly significant. It represents fertile ideas that exist within you and the potential for you to use them (likely soon!) in order to change your circumstances for the better. In reverse, the Empress signifies a blockage to your creative expression.

Upside-down, this card represents impotence, infertility, poverty, repressed truth, and lack of what is, in essence, the Empress herself. With these blockages in place, you will struggle to achieve the abundance the Empress wants to offer you. Look to the surrounding cards for clues regarding how to remove these blockages!

4. The Emperor. The Emperor card represents the quintessential divine masculine. It is about power, fatherhood, leadership, protection, order, and successful accomplishments. Pulling this card in a reading suggests that success is imminent. As long as you use the strength of your will and your clear, focused intellect, you can achieve anything you set your mind to. This card can also represent a father figure or paternal entity in your life that you may or may not be getting along well with. In reverse, the Emperor signifies what happens when authority is lost.

Perhaps tyranny occurs — perhaps unproductive revolution. Perhaps lack of center and perhaps additional strength. The outcome is up to you. Furthermore, this reversal can represent the loss of a father figure, lack of focus, indecision, or lack of self-worth in relation to your dreams. It could also be a clue that you've been overly judgmental against others recently.

5. The Hierophant. The Hierophant card represents the importance of learning, tradition, and routine. This card will appear in a reading to remind you to take counsel of those you trust most before making major decisions. Furthermore, it will remind you to value those people whose counsel you utterly trust. The Hierophant encourages the following of established traditions, but he also accepts that there is a limitation in tradition that some cannot withstand. For those individuals, this card represents what may stand in your way to success. For those who accept and embrace tradition, this card represents the beginning of your journey to self-actualization. In reverse, the Hierophant signifies what happens when tradition goes out the window: chaos, rebellion, and free-flow of wisdom. While this situation may sound entirely beneficial to some, structure in the sharing of wisdom is much preferred to free-flow, and systems are more effective when they're in place than they are when they're in ruins. Watch out for rejection or a shifting in values.

6. The Lovers. The card of the Lovers represents that love is headed your way. However, it insists that you cannot handle love if you're not able to first love and appreciate yourself. The Lovers can be a signal that your twin flame is headed into your life, but it could also represent the urgent need for you to fall in love with yourself as your own twin flame. This card insists we appreciate the logic that the heart holds dear, for it is more valuable than many could ever imagine. In reverse, the Lovers signify that struggles in love are ahead. Whether it's indecision, jealousy, unrequited or chaotic love, separation, or impotence, something's about to be disturbed in your romantic haven. If you don't have a partner, it could be that some issues are arising in your personality that are keeping you from experiencing self-love. Look to surrounding cards for clues as to how you can fix the situation.

7. The Chariot. The Chariot card signifies that any issues you're working through will be resolved in a short time. It suggests that embracing control of your life will allow you to find both the peace and the change you desire in the situation. The Chariot insists on growth, mastery, success, triumph, journeying, development, and understanding. However, none of this success can happen without first struggling through conflict, so the Chariot card also assumes that trials have happened recently (or are happening) that will soon be resolved. The Chariot shows how even a successful person is a work in progress. In reverse, the Chariot signifies interruptions in your path to success or blatant failures that stand in your way. It can also symbolize a loss of, or general lack of, control that leads to burnout. This card can represent upcoming danger, but it's often a danger that will only affect your personality. Without careful consideration and alteration to your circumstances, you will stagnate, and your growth will be disastrously interrupted.

8. Strength. The Strength card – with its image of a brave woman standing beside a large beast – demonstrates the peace of the Goddess that exists within every person. Both men and women have goddess blessings within that express as patience, understanding, compassion, and charisma. This card signals that those blessings are present and working to your advantage. Furthermore, Strength signifies the importance of faith and courage, even for feminine individuals. Strength reminds us all to get back in touch with our inner wildness in order to honor our highest selves. In reverse, Strength signifies a lack of courage that borders on fear. Instead of being brave and accessing one's blessings, this card in reverse symbolizes that one is experiencing torment, hopelessness, and failed integrations (of any lessons the universe has presented). If you pull Strength in reverse, look out for places in your life where weakness or indecision could be holding you back, find stillness, and carefully examine your emotions and thoughts for clues about how to move forward.

9. The Hermit. The Hermit card is a powerful indicator that intense transformation lies ahead, but it also suggests that you will need to spend serious time alone to embrace that transformative path. The Hermit forces you to face those spiritual and emotional elements in your life that are likely holding you back. Furthermore, this card reminds you of your connection to your higher self. Once you access that alone time, this connection will be both strengthened and developed so that it's more useful to you than ever. If you pull the Hermit card, it's time to withdraw, get introspective, and retreat into your own psyche for a little while. When you re-emerge, you will be like a butterfly emerging from its caterpillar cocoon. In reverse, the Hermit signifies the worst that can happen with alone time: isolation, ostracism, fear, loneliness, and stagnation. If you pull the Hermit in reverse, look closely at your social patterns to see if you've been too isolated to sustain growth. Sometimes, this alone time starts out healthy and turns toxic, as with moments after betrayal, crisis, or breakup. To ensure things remain productive, embrace this shadow time as a temporary thing that will inevitably lead to growth, rather than seeing it as a moment to inhabit for eternity.

10. The Wheel of Fortune. The Wheel of Fortune card suggests that bounty is coming! It shows how you can reap the rewards of your current situation by channeling prosperity and by embracing inevitability. To receive this card in a reading means that one season of the self is ending to make way for the next, more powerful season. The Wheel of Fortune represents the Hermit's wisdom, and introspection put into action. It's the next step after the Hermit's necessary isolation, which is the actualization of the individual's soul mission. In reverse, the Wheel of Fortune signifies that you're being faced with change but fiercely ignoring it. This card shows how your internal harvest may have been bittersweet (or perhaps more bitter than sweet whatsoever) rather than productive. Additionally, there may be more difficult times ahead before you're able to grow. The trick to the situation may be allowing yourself the freedom to let go of what no longer serves.

11. Justice. The Justice card represents that there's a clear path to success in your

vicinity. You'll have to access balance and clarity, however, in order to find that path. Furthermore, you'll have to learn, intimately, your own truth. Those who pull Justice should know that an important dilemma will surface in your life shortly, and your choice will determine so much. Make sure that you're actively *choosing* in response to the dilemma rather than just *reacting* to the options instinctually. Take the time to think things out and embrace what is truly best. In reverse, Justice signifies the existence of imbalance, dishonesty, and unfairness in reference to both the self and others. If you pull this card, look to your life to find what's causing imbalance. Open a wide, discerning, introspective eye toward yourself to see where injustice or unfairness may be controlling your actions unintentionally.

12. The Hanged Man. The Hanged Man card represents your experience becoming intensified, refocused, deepened, or expanded. The Hanged Man on the card hangs upside-down, and this positioning represents a paradigm shift and a complete perspective upheaval. However, this shifting and upheaval is nothing but positive. If you draw this card, your future holds a huge reversal that will draw good things and progress your way. Expect upheavals, shifting, and transformations, but don't be afraid! By drawing this card, it signifies that you may even be set to experience a shaman-style initiation into the secrets of the universe after you emerge from the phase of the Hanged Man.

In reverse, the Hanged Man signifies the inability to adjust to a new paradigm. Receiving this card in a reading could indicate that you're fighting progress, that you're playing the victim, or that you're not self-aware enough to handle the transitions ahead. Tune deeply into your thoughts and try to experiment by playing devil's advocate with yourself as much as possible. Turn your life on its head for a resolution to this issue.

13. Death. The Death card is not as literal as you might think, and I strongly discourage you from feeling scared or frustrated when you draw this card! Death is one of the most inspiring and positive cards in the deck, as a matter of fact. Death signifies full-on transformation. One must submerge into the depths of the self before he or she can rise up with new power. Consider the images of the Phoenix, the resurrection, and the initiation. When you draw this card, it suggests that you may be about to greet your shadow side. But if you do, you'll be remade stronger, more powerful, and more passionate about your goals than ever before. Prepare for intensity, passion, and the shedding of what doesn't serve you. In reverse, Death signifies that you're about to greet your shadow side, but the outcome may not be as beneficial as you'd like unless you change a few things. For now, this card in reverse suggests that you're likely to meet your shadow with fear, which could lead to stagnation, exhaustion, and pessimism. As you move forward, stay open to what's to come and agree to forgive yourself to avoid the worst.

14. Temperance. The card of Temperance signifies potential for magic, lasting peace, and pain transmuted into positivity. This card is a very hopeful one to draw in any reading. If you do draw Temperance, it likely means that you've just emerged from a period of great upheaval, or it could suggest that you have just come to incredible new knowledge about yourself in a spiritual sense. What you do with this enhanced knowledge is what can be likened to magic. In reverse, Temperance signifies that you're in a state of imbalance. You've lost track of your path and your center, and you may have been extra argumentative with others recently, too. You're likely feeling fragmented or torn in disparate directions, and you'll need to bring yourself back together before you can achieve any sense of harmony. Look to the surrounding cards to find out how to go about that.

15. The Devil. Despite its name, this card – like the Death card – appears more terrifying than it actually is. Drawing this card does not mean you're possessed or doomed in any sense. It *can* mean, however, that you're being controlled by something external or material that you'd be better off free from. Consider how you're being repressed or obsessed by things outside yourself. Consider how you're being controlled or limited by some potential addiction (whether it be to drugs, alcohol, cigarettes, coffee, shopping, stealing, etc.). The Devil card points out how you've been shackled, and it reminds you how important it is to reclaim your own power of will. In reverse, the Devil signifies what you likely feared from the Devil card itself: detrimental circumstances, abuse of power, devastating unhappiness, lack of self-control to temptation, and the (re)surfacing of one's inner demons. If you draw this card, be very cautious about how you proceed. If you aim for growth, many things will need to change.

16. The Tower. The Tower card suggests that you remained imprisoned by the Devil card and had to fight your way out. Traditionally, the Tower represents strife, conflict, destruction, devastation, and utter despair; however, I see the Tower as a bit more hopeful. If you draw the Tower, it means that you've decided to fight for something you believe in, and you're destroying everything left of that toxicity in order to succeed in your fight. The destruction comes from your liberation. The upheaval comes from immense and instant illumination. The beauty of creation awaits you once more as soon as your struggles settle.

In reverse, the Tower signifies that the concept of illumination may have been frightening or daunting to you. It suggests that you've shut yourself up in the tower, rather than broken free from it. Furthermore, concepts of imprisonment and avoidance of responsibility abound when pulling this card. If you do draw the Tower reversed in a reading, remember to release all fear and proceed as bravely and confidently as possible.

17. The Star. The Star card represents a beautiful and transcendent openness that

results from true illumination. This card suggests the happy resolution to all the events signified by the Tower. Furthermore, the Star contains the potential for wholeness, lasting healing, and completion of detrimental cycles. If you draw this card in your reading, be proud yet calm and hopeful! Good things are coming your way. In reverse, the Star signifies what can happen when the Tower in reverse advances in time: stagnation, waste of time, loss of self-respect, and loss of intuitive potential. If you shut yourself down to the potential for illumination, it's not surprising that you'll have likewise shut yourself down to progress and growth. Breathe deeply and believe in yourself as you move forward with this knowledge.

18. The Moon. The Moon card takes a step beyond what's happened with the Star and asserts the querent as a fully-functioning psychic-in-training. If you draw this card, embrace the divine feminine in your life and devote yourself to your truth. Be unafraid to greet your shadow self, for your dark reflection is still that: *your reflection.* You may withdraw from society for a time (or you may be in that period now), but that withdrawal does not mean isolation, for you will be (or are) spiritually journeying the entire time. Keep an eye on your dreams and remember that your imagination can do incredible things.

In reverse, the Moon signifies a state of confusion brought about by being unable to integrate your newfound faith or spirituality. If you draw this card, you likely feel uncomfortable with the concept or action of imagination. You may be relying on substances for your spiritual growth, too. There may have been signs pointing you in different directions, but you haven't followed them yet. To heal your current path, you'll need to proceed carefully. Look inside yourself for answers.

19. The Sun. The Sun card represents what the sun typically symbolizes: joy, freedom, happiness, carefree energy, expansiveness, wonder, and success. Furthermore, this card suggests that you've begun to follow your path to enlightenment, and you're currently feeling the focus and clarity to fully achieve your dreams (as long as you stay on this path!). Remain optimistic and be unafraid to share what you've learned with others! Knowledge is light, after all.

In reverse, the Sun signifies that your inner light has dimmed. Perhaps you've refused to share your knowledge with others. Perhaps you're unable to see things clearly. Perhaps you're arrogant and assume you don't need to know more. Whatever your circumstances are, you doubt yourself or your path to some degree, and it's negatively affecting your psyche.

However, this card could simply suggest that the success you crave is merely delayed.

20. Judgment. The card of Judgment is another card of rebirth. It insists that there will be a whole new set of paths to follow after you're settled in that energy of the Sun card. When one door closes, so many more open. Judgment also signifies that a time for decision-making is at hand. There are many changes ahead, and you'll be tested to see if you can carry your frequency of light. Make the decisions that best reflect your truth in order to succeed. In reverse, Judgment signifies that you've heard the call to act, to change, and to become reborn, but the trouble is that you've ignored it. You may not be ready to understand what's at hand, but you could also just be willfully ignorant. If you pull this card, consider how you may be acting out of a fear of change.

21. The World. The World card is another in the tarot that symbolizes completion. Those who draw this card have gone through periods of great success that brought lasting satisfaction and pride. The World card is about celebration. It's about the dancing done when you've achieved all that you hoped for. It's about the festivities – the union of self and world – that occur when one's in his or her prime. The World demonstrates that abundance (if not currently achieved) is nearer than you think! Keep your chin up and be patient. You won't have to wait much longer.

In reverse, the World signifies delay of success. There may be limitations in place, or you could feel like you're in a state of suspended animation. If you're feeling anything but validated and free, it's likely that your most important work is not completed quite yet. If this card is pulled, I recommend waiting out the situation, for movement and progress will absolutely return in time.

22. The Fool

The Fool both opens and closes the Major Arcana, and that's because it associates most strongly with innocence, openness, and new beginnings. The Fool represents both closure and conception. It's a card of balanced extremes and energy focused through playfulness. If you've drawn the Fool, it could be because you're acting like one, but it could also be because you need to take a less serious route in life in order to succeed. Remember to laugh at yourself! Take yourself less seriously and play a little more! Optimism comes to those who maintain good humor.

In reverse, the Fool signifies that you're playing out the worst qualities of the card. You're childlike, playful, and extreme, yes. But you're also naïve, irrational, and foolhardy. Don't be afraid of change! Don't let yourself be trapped by routine either! You may be naïve and gullible now, but your awareness of these traits is pivotal knowledge to be able to change them in the future.

Minor Arcana

The Minor Arcana, also called the Lesser Arcana, represents personality aspects and struggles or experiences that exist for all humanity in this world. The Minor Arcana is divided into 16 court or face cards and 40 "pip" or numbered cards from ace to 10. These 56 cards are all also divided into 4 suits or elemental types. Sometimes the suits are called different things, but I've noted where that terminology may differ for your convenience.

Wands (a.k.a. – Clubs / Batons / Staves)

Wands, Clubs, Batons, and Staves all represent the same energy. This suit is all about passion, inspiration, initiation, impulsiveness, action, physical sensation, and strength-building. Wands often signify what is generated in order to inspire others. Furthermore, they're associated with summertime.

Ace of Wands

The Ace of Wands is all about birth, new action, and expression of creative energy. Those who draw this card are unerringly gifted with a creative energy of some type, and they're likely to have the vigor to express that gift soon (if they haven't already). Sometimes, this card also represents recent conception or the upcoming birth of a child.

In reverse, this card signifies that there's a blockage in your energy, creative or otherwise. As long as you're aware of this blockage, it's soon to pass.

2 of Wands

The 2 of Wands symbolizes a tension that may be blocking that free-flow of creativity. How do you feel about your work? Are you truly satisfied in your life? This card encourages you to examine what might be holding you back. Once you figure out what it is, you will have established a doorway that will change your circumstances once it is opened.

In reverse, this card signifies a sudden release of tension which can translate into a creative work of genius.

3 of Wands

The 3 of Wands shows you how hard you've been working. You probably didn't need the confirmation, but your higher self wants you to know that he or she has noticed all the effort you've been putting in. Rewards are coming, and a whole new path may be revealed in a short time. Maintain confidence and direction for your goals are within reach!

In reverse, this card signifies that you may have been following a dream that's just not right for you – at least not right now. Think deeply about your goals and see if you can find the one that's misaligned from your truth. Another meaning of this card in reverse is that you've been focusing too much on the past in order to move into your own future.

4 of Wands

The 4 of Wands shows that the effort you've put into building a happy home has paid off. Things are feeling supportive, stabilized, comforting, and rewarding. You have a sense that you're settled enough with your life and your family to start the major project you've been putting off for so long. You're proud, joyful, and ready for what the world has in store.

In reverse, this card signifies much of the same as the right-side-up version. The only difference is that you may have a temporary break from your work that's caused by a delay in action. If you experience this break, take full advantage of it. Rest up for what's to come.

5 of Wands

The 5 of Wands symbolizes playful conflict on the horizon. There's an interplay of activities and minds that's been surrounding you, but there may be an interruption to – or heightening of – that energy soon. Stand firm in your truth and open yourself up to the possibility for a sexual liaison (if you're into it!) because it could be the right time with that special someone.

In reverse, this card signifies conflict experienced internally. There could also be a degree of mistrust against oneself that's been holding you back. Turn to meditation to reestablish your trust in yourself and look to the surrounding cards in your spread to receive clues about the situation as a whole.

6 of Wands

The 6 of Wands represents recent victory achieved through focused and sustained effort. It demonstrates that you have the capacity to be a leader (once you're ready to embrace that role). Furthermore, the 6 of Wands reveals your potential for fame. Any actions you undertake towards your goal will end up successful as long as this card is in play.

In reverse, this card signifies how disastrous distrust can be. It can derail you from your path, it can shut off connections to others, and it can eliminate potential positions. If you've let distrust infect your heart and mind, it's time to work for resolution. On the other hand, if you see distrust creeping into your life right now, try to get to the root of the issue and eradicate it before it gets stuck in you for good.

7 of Wands

The 7 of Wands reveals struggles on your horizon. There may be challenges to your authority that you don't appreciate, or it could just be that you're not feeling properly respected in your line of work. If you draw this card, proceed with caution and try to discern the biggest obstacles in your life through meditation. Once they're discovered, you can process these obstacles yourself without bringing the issue to others (and that would just make matters so much worse anyway).

In reverse, this card signifies that you're feeling some emotional turmoil over your work situation. Maybe someone has criticized your work, and you're frustrated or embarrassed. Maybe someone has told you the boss is checking on your work and you're extra stressed. Regardless of the situation, try not to let other peoples' concerns weigh you down. Work to your highest capacity and remember to live your truth if you're ready to settle this imbalance.

8 of Wands

The 8 of Wands card is all about speed, accuracy, and aim. This card signals that you're like an arrow shot expertly toward its target. You're swiftly approaching all you hope for so strongly, and anything you attempt at this time is bound to be efficient, successful, serendipitous, and exciting. Don't get caught up in the vibe! Try to use this energy for actualization and action.

In reverse, this card signifies that something is ending for you. Feelings of foreboding, concern, and frustration abound for you right now, and you fear losing things (and people) that mean the most to you. In order to succeed and not flounder, it may be difficult, but all it takes is an attitude check to shift things in the right direction.

9 of Wands

The 9 of Wands symbolizes a moment of lull for you. You've just been through some nonsense, and the conflict is still playing out in your heart and mind. Because of this recent conflict and any lingering tensions, you may be feeling fearful or unsure of your future. You may be more antisocial or shy than ever, and it's unlikely that you're willing to take on big, life-altering action. However, this card encourages you to go for it! Let go of the pain and dive back into the experience! You never know what beautiful outcomes will arise.

In reverse, this card signifies that you're intensely working away at an internal issue. Whatever you've noticed within yourself that you don't like, you've decided to eradicate it. However, the issue is a bit more ingrained in you than you initially thought! Have hope and be stubborn! Try a different approach to the situation! If that doesn't work, the surrounding cards in this reading may provide the clues you need for resolution.

10 of Wands

The 10 of Wands focuses on feelings of overwork. You've put a lot of effort into your vocation or a project of choice, and you're desperate to start seeing rewards. If you work for someone else, it could be that they're asking too much of you. If you are self-employed, it could be that you're tackling too much. Be careful not to burn yourself out, but know that if you do, another path to success will emerge to direct you in time.

In reverse, this card signifies the potential for freedom. It could be that a new path is opening up for you, but it could also be that an old path is burning and crumbling before your eyes. Keep an eye open for clues in your life that can direct you to this liberating path. Over time, you will achieve balance and just reward.

Page of Wands

The Page of Wands insists that a young and energetic person may be about to enter your life. This person will provide needed inspiration to your life, and he or she may signify a new phase of your own life about to begin. Things are about to pick up for you!

In reverse, this card signifies that someone who's overly confused or uncertain may enter your life instead. You may need to serve as an example for them so that you both aren't distracted to the point of stagnation. Remember to remain energetic and resolute despite this (person's) energy.

Knight of Wands

The Knight of Wands reminds you of the passion and eagerness that can accompany pure and fresh ideas. You might have been feeling listless or directionless lately, but that's all about to change. It could be a person that inspires you or a philosophy or a course of action. Whatever it is, it will provide challenges that help you grow exponentially. All you needed was a little bit of rebellious information to inspire you!

In reverse, this card signifies that you lack the energy you need to either act or think appropriately. As much as possible, be sure not to lie, not to lose your temper, not to control people, and not to ignore your passions. It's time to live authentically and fruitfully!

Queen of Wands

The Queen of Wands suggests that a wise, generous, and creative feminine presence is about to enter your life. It can mean that you're about to channel this energy for yourself, too. Don't shy away from femininity, charity, altruism, or compassion at this time! Be brave and express your willingness to help others. Volunteerism is a great practice at this time.

In reverse, this card signifies that you, someone else, or your mentality are about to take away from the freedoms of others. Make sure that your goals don't detract from the lives of others when you pull this card. Double-check your intentions, too. It can't hurt to reexamine them once in a while regardless.

King of Wands

The King of Wands symbolizes a person, opinion, or philosophy that's perfected through effort and hardened through passion. In your life, this card could represent troubling or stressful negotiations with others. Furthermore, it could signify a financial settlement that's about to be decided in your favor. Finally, the King of Wands suggests that it's time to take up the limelight and own your hard-earned successes.

In reverse, this card signifies that the hopefulness, direction, eagerness, enthusiasm, passion, and intensity of the King of Wands has been focused toward either extreme positive or extreme negative expression. Don't let other people tear you down, but don't do that same thing to others either! This card teaches the value of love and sacrifice in protection and progress, respectively.

Swords

Swords are all about intellect, mentalism, thoughtfulness, analytical thinking, concrete planning, and even deceitful scheming. Swords often signify what is sensed intuitively and then developed intellectually. They are also associated with springtime.

Ace of Swords

The Ace of Swords represents mental clarity as well as success on the horizon. It suggests that you've been given a gift of intellect, and it encourages you to use that gift to the advantage of all others. There are incredible opportunities available to you in your field as long as you show confidence in yourself and your craft.

In reverse, this card signifies that you're experiencing imbalance or harshness on your journey related to overreliance on judgment. Remember that others are a reflection of you and that separation is an illusion in order to reestablish balance.

2 of Swords

The 2 of Swords predicts an opposition in your future. Whether it's between you and someone else or between two other people, there's conflict and strife ahead. You may be asked to be the mediator if you're not too personally involved in the situation. If you draw this card, double-check yourself to be sure not to put off your responsibilities to others.

In reverse, this card signifies internal conflict, tension, and self-deceit. Devote yourself to your truth in order to change the situation.

3 of Swords

The 3 of Swords isn't the most positive card to pull. It represents a time of great heartache. It could be that you've recently experienced a breakup, or you might just be in a phase of personal transformation. Regardless of the reason, your heart is torn apart by some sort of conflict. Let these emotions fill you and don't avoid them – they will help you grow in ways you could never imagine (at least, not right now).

In reverse, this card signifies that an old wound may be re-opened soon. It may already be raw and re-opened right now. Allow yourself to forgive whoever wronged you, and don't let yourself get caught up in feelings of woundedness or victimhood. Take the high road.

4 of Swords

The 4 of Swords represents the importance of discernment. You may be about to face (or you're currently facing) an intense conflict, and you'll need to make sure you confront those who deserve it while retreating from others who don't. You'll need to make sure that you're aligned with your stable foundation of truth in order to stay above the struggles. Meditation may help you be able to keep the peace.

In reverse, this card signifies that you're ready to come back into the world after a period of isolation. You've been hurt, but you're healing, so you emerge armed with positive energy for the future.

5 of Swords

The 5 of Swords warns you that you're coming up against hardship. There will be struggle ahead, and you may not turn out to be the victor. There may be threats to your dignity or failures in tests of loyalty. There may be a breakdown of communication between friends or lovers that proves toxic, and you'll have to remain open and willing to improve in order to find closure with this issue.

In reverse, this card signifies feelings of despair that fill you. These feelings have surfaced due to a defeat you recently suffered. Allow yourself to be forgiven, and instead of wallowing, follow the path to renewal.

6 of Swords

The 6 of Swords shares important information about peace. It reveals that peace can come from the sharing of differences with others. Truth is not consistent. It is subjective, individual, and largely underappreciated, which is why it's so important for each of us to share our truths with others. This sharing increases the collective capacity for empathy, understanding, and growth. By drawing this card, you've shown that you're ready to move beyond separation from others to a place of intellectual solidarity that's achieved through appreciation of difference.

In reverse, this card signifies the pain you sense in confrontation. Sometimes, confrontation is so painful that we put it off for months, if not years. Sometimes, confrontation is so overwhelming that you get stuck and refuse to process the pain behind the circumstance. Pulling this card means that you must face the issue or resolve it within yourself in order to move forward.

7 of Swords

The 7 of Swords is a card to be very excited about! It suggests that magical knowledge is just past your fingertips. You may be about to embark on a voyage of great learning – or it could be that your spirit guides are about to "take you to school" to relearn your basics before growth can be achieved. Regardless, there's a definite air of excitement in your life, and new veins of knowledge shine out to you in the darkness.

In reverse, this card signifies a number of things. It could be that you're about to help someone out, rework a previous conflict, receive previously stolen goods, use your words against someone, or experience intense trickery or deception. Regardless, things are about to get weird, and the essence of mystery stands firm throughout any upcoming struggles.

8 of Swords

The 8 of Swords represents a tricky situation that you likely feel stuck in. Whether it's due to your circumstances or the needs of another person, you're restricted, tied down, and focused on thinking through fear. Try to remember that fear is just a mindset (and an unproductive one, at that!). Focus instead on using your mind to establish your own liberation, and you should be able to find the silver lining to the situation in no time.

In reverse, this card signifies that a time of escape or entrapment is almost over for you. You see freedom on the horizon, and you're willing to do anything to achieve that freedom. Ignore gossip and drama that wants to stand in your way, and then you're sure to succeed.

9 of Swords

The 9 of Swords represents that you may be deep in a period of darkness, internally. Although things may look alright on the outside, on the inside, you're experiencing anguish, despair, and utter devastation. You could be experiencing the powerful and formative moment that many call the "Dark Night of the Soul." Remember that you're not as alone as you think you are and keep your sights on your goals! Don't lose track of your truth in this state, for the outcome can be an identity crisis.

In reverse, this card signifies one of two things. First, it could be that your truth is being used against your will in ways you're uncomfortable with (i.e., as a scapegoat for blame or as an avatar for someone's ethnic or religious hatred). Second, it could be that troubling situations are about to get much better. Either way, expect blunt realizations and potential for deep transformations.

10 of Swords

The 10 of Swords represents the lowest point you can reach, but it also realizes that the lowest lows occur right before the brightest dawns. If you're feeling dejected, misdirected, undervalued, inferior, or betrayed right now, know that things *will* be okay in time. Things may end for you on the short-term, but that will open up avenues for success in the long-term. Remember that things tend to happen in 3s and proceed with as little hatred as possible.

In reverse, this card signifies that you've made a deep and lasting realization recently regarding your perceptions of life. You used to think things unfair or unbalanced or frustrating, but you've just accepted that you have the power to change your reality. Look inside and heal conflicts on that level to see what reverberates into more external realms.

Page of Swords

The Page of Swords could represent you (or someone else) who's having trouble with communication. New lessons for this person are about to arise, but he or she will have to practice in order to establish fluency and eloquence. It could also be that incredible conversations are coming your way! Don't be afraid to start up a discussion with a stranger.

In reverse, this card signifies that you (or someone near you) is being too detached in life. Get close to others and be unafraid of forming bonds! However, be careful not to become too controlling of others at this time.

Knight of Swords

The Knight of Swords is all about revolutionary intelligence. You may be about to meet a person or encounter a theory or philosophy that's completely radical. It (or he/she) will challenge everything you thought you knew, and you'll emerge smarter and stronger. You may be about to embark on travel through the air.

In reverse, this card signifies that you're approaching something in the wrong way. Whether it's a person, a thing, or a situation, you're just not coming at it quite right. Be selfless and reject urges for control, aggression, or abuse whenever they arise.

Queen of Swords

The Queen of Swords reveals the presence of someone feminine who's devoted to justice. This person may be about to enter your life, or it could be you who's about to step up to the plate. Furthermore, this card can simply signal a shift of attitude from subjectivity to objectivity for the sake of the greater good.

In reverse, this card signifies a feminine energy that's devoted to justice but who's suffered greatly at the hands of the system. Pulling this card can mean that you, your philosophy on life, or someone else close to you has become embittered to the point of detachment from social spheres. Bitterness is a disease that can be cured by connection with others, so fight this frustration with love!

King of Swords

The King of Swords is all about legal, medical, scientific, or financial advancement. It could represent a person high-up in any one of these fields, but it could also suggest that you hold this potential with yourself. When you pull this card, look to the areas in *your* own life that could use a better foundation. Especially be wary of unsteady backgrounds in terms of justice, self-sufficiency, honesty, and intellect.

In reverse, this card signifies that even the purest goals can be twisted with impure intention. It reminds you to check your strategy so that you're not hurting anyone, intentionally or not. Furthermore, this card encourages you to communicate your truth *tactfully* to others. Otherwise, you may come up against intense and long-lasting conflict over your word choice.

Cups (a.k.a. – Chalices)

Cups and Chalices both represent the same energy. This suit is about emotionality, the sensual world, creativity and growth, and wateriness. Cups often signify what is felt deeply and encouraged toward others. Furthermore, they're associated with autumnal times of the year.

Ace of Cups

The Ace of Cups symbolizes the blossoming of romantic intention. Essentially, it reveals the potential for new emotional interests related to creation, inspiration, or romance. There are new relationships of all sorts on the horizon, or it could be that your relationship with something or someone is about to be kicked up a notch.

In reverse, this card signifies that you're experiencing a lull in romance or creative inspiration. If you find yourself drawing this card, ask yourself what you may have recently rejected that would have actually served you well.

2 of Cups

The 2 of Cups demonstrates prosperous and amorous times ahead! Those seeking romance or healing will find their wishes fulfilled, and those seeking reconciliation with others will also find their hopes confirmed. The 2 of Cups reveals how love can be a powerful force for healing in so many ways.

In reverse, this card signifies pain induced from love gone awry. Your emotions are intense, and they can drag you down into your own depths, but rest easy knowing that satisfaction *will* come into your life again.

3 of Cups

The 3 of Cups symbolizes a lively, celebratory time filled with glee, love, and togetherness. This card represents shared joy over gifts that will benefit the community. You may have just made it through a troubling time, or it may be time to harvest the fruits of your hard work. Regardless of the cause, give yourself to the revelry! Treat yourself! You deserve it.

In reverse, this card signifies the worst aspects of a life filled with partying: overindulgence, overspending, and superficiality. Make sure you satisfy your inner needs as well as your external ones in order to correct this imbalance.

4 of Cups

The 4 of Cups represents a period in which your emotions or your daily "flow" feel out of balance or interrupted. You may have overworked yourself recently, which could be causing this imbalance. It could also be that your best friendships and/or your partnership feel off-kilter, making everything else out of whack. If you're feeling stagnant or indifferent, try to bask in the comforts that surround you. Positivity is the trick to escaping this mood.

In reverse, this card signifies that you're ready to move on from this period of stagnation and indifference! Your energy has been redirected, and after all you've been through, you're ready to once again take on the world.

5 of Cups

The 5 of Cups represents a complication added to your standard emotional satisfaction. You likely weren't expecting this complication, and you're unsure how to respond to it. Feelings of abandonment, surprise, fear, worthlessness, and loss arise, but you know that they're not the norm for you. You could be holding on to the past too harshly. Look to the present and future in order to heal this wound.

In reverse, this card signifies that you've suffered immensely, but you've reached the perfect time to move forward. It's a great time to resolve unfinished business with others or to reassess a conflict from the past. Keep an open heart and remember the value of mercy.

6 of Cups

The 6 of Cups symbolizes (re)union, gatherings, and exchanges. This card reveals the importance of love across time and space, for you may be about to reunite with unknown family, old friends, previous lovers, or embittered rivals from the past. It's time to rehash those old relationships and find out how they helped you grow (even if it didn't feel like growth at the time).

In reverse, this card signifies trials involved with revisiting one's past. You may find that wounds you thought had healed are actually still quite raw. You might find that reunion experiences don't end up as productive as you'd hoped. If you draw this card, take things slowly, and don't put yourself through too much emotional stress anytime soon.

7 of Cups

The 7 of Cups suggests that you have a lot on your mind. Numerous goals and dreams are competing for focus in your head, and therefore, no path rings true, and no dreams feel 100% worth following. Be patient throughout this period of scattered energy, for focus will return in time. For the time being, entertain all these possible dreams and play them out in your head (rather than in real life) to see how realistic they actually are.

In reverse, this card signifies that you've delayed your decision-making either too long or exactly the right amount of time. Therefore, this card could represent a missed opportunity, or it could suggest that you're right on schedule, using your will power to achieve your goals with perfection.

8 of Cups

The 8 of Cups suggests that it might be time for you to move on. You've dedicated a lot of your energy recently (or over the past few years) to a relationship that's become unproductive. Don't ignore that truth anymore: things are now utterly and unavoidably *unproductive*. It's time to step away. It's time to move on, and that may seem harsh, but I promise that new growth will replace what you've lost.

In reverse, this card signifies that you're going through a rough point in your current romantic relationship. You're considering the pros and cons, and you're thinking of what it would be like to be single (or with someone else) again. You may be thinking this so often that you're exhausted of it by now. It's not likely that action will result from these thoughts at this time.

9 of Cups

The 9 of Cups signifies that something you've worked very hard to attain is finally within grasp. It represents satisfaction, contentment, and deep and lasting happiness. The 9 of Cups also suggests that any conflicts that arise around this time will be easily defused. Finally, this card represents the potential for laziness and stagnation if you wallow in this success for too long without establishing a new path.

As always, the ending of one thing must correlate to the beginning of another. Keep your efforts focused on that next up-swing.

In reverse, this card signifies how something that used to stand in your way is now resolved. Whether it was yourself, something, or someone else, whatever was holding you back is just about conquered. Make sure you're not overindulging during this time, as it can hinder your ability to finalize this conquest.

10 of Cups

The 10 of Cups symbolizes emotional fulfillment. Everything you hoped for yourself now feels within reach, and you're brimming with love for both yourself and others. This card is extremely hopeful, as it encourages you to reach for the stars. In success-filled moments, don't forget to keep dreaming! This card will remind you of what's possible when you think you've achieved all your wishes.

In reverse, this card signifies that there may be struggles at home. Whether it's with your family or your intimate partner, things are decidedly rocky. It could be that someone's leaving home, and you're having trouble adjusting. Keep an open heart and embrace the change that you face rather than fighting it. It may seem unfathomable, but you will adjust in time.

Page of Cups

The Page of Cups demonstrates a new direction for creativity. You might be starting a new artistic venture, or you may be about to bring a baby into this world! New things are starting up everywhere, and you'll have to make sure your cup is brimming with love if you plan to take it all in.

In reverse, this card signifies hardship associated with love or creative direction. You may have all the urge to succeed, but your emotions or actions could disagree. It could be that you're confused about what you actually need from your art, from yourself, from your job, and/or from others. Start meditating to find the answer or look to the surrounding cards for clues.

Knight of Cups

The Knight of Cups represents either a person or an attitude that's idealistic, hopeful, romantic, and dreamy. Be careful not to be too naïve in your dreams and ideals, however, for some things are not as easy to manifest as you'd think. You might be about to use your healing abilities to help others, but you also might be about to engage in travel over water. This card has many meanings.

In reverse, this card signifies that something (or someone) is hiding from you in plain sight. Be true to yourself, and make sure you're not the one hiding! Bring your secrets out of the darkness, and clean any skeletons out of your closet. It's time for some emotional spring-cleaning if you're hoping for growth.

Queen of Cups

The Queen of Cups symbolizes a person in your life who is truly devoted to loving you. This person is likely *not* your partner. More often than not, it's a teacher, a parent, a guardian, or a therapist (regardless of gender) whose interactions with you are more nurturing than anything else. This person will be of increasing importance to you in the near future. This card can also suggest that your creative dreams are about to be actualized.

In reverse, this card signifies one's struggles to feel comfortable in a new social setting. Things have changed recently, but you're not adjusting well. You're unsure, guarded, alienated, and uncomfortable. Try to channel happiness often, and work on healing your deepest emotional wounds in order to correct this imbalance.

King of Cups

The King of Cups demonstrates that a sensitive, spiritual, and emotional masculine person may be about to enter your life, but it can also suggest that a new spiritual (or artistic) path is about to be revealed to you instead. Look out for jobs (or people interested) in the fields of publishing, music, art, or theatre.

In reverse, this card signifies that your partner (or potential partner) is too distracted to be able to love you (or him or herself) fully. It could be that he or she is caught off-guard by the relationship, but it's more likely that it's a substance abuse issue. This card is both a warning and an opportunity for transformation.

Pentacles (a.k.a. – Coins / Rings / Discs)

Pentacles, Coins, Rings, and Discs all represent the same energy. This suit is all about materialism, home life, and earthiness. Pentacles often signify what is realized and then put into action. Furthermore, they're associated with wintery times of the year.

Ace of Pentacles

The Ace of Pentacles suggests that financial gain is on your horizon! There is a hint of something prosperous starting up for you soon. Furthermore, you may feel a sense of deep peace at this time with respect to your job, your relationships, and your home life. However, it could be that only *one* of these aspects of your life evokes this serene sensation.

In reverse, this card signifies how you may be controlled by vice. Greed, lust, addiction, envy, and sloth are most likely to be the vice in question. Let go of any unnecessary attachments in order to heal this issue.

2 of Pentacles

The 2 of Pentacles symbolizes the need for trust in upcoming trying times. You may feel instinctually that you should proceed with caution, but that urge is not actually the best option for you right now. Open yourself to the universe and to the possibilities that others will offer. Find a balance between intellect and play, and remember to trust in the process.

In reverse, this card signifies that what you're trying to balance or juggle isn't exactly working out. You risk losing money and resources if you follow the path you've been on. Proceed with caution.

3 of Pentacles

The 3 of Pentacles shows you how you've actualized the fruits of your labor! All that you've been working on will soon be finalized, and you'll receive all the necessary compensation and praise shortly, so be patient! If you have the sense to improve the work you've done, follow that intuition! It will likely develop your project to an even more advanced (and prosperous) level.

In reverse, this card signifies that laziness (or fear) has gotten in the way of your success. Your projects stand incomplete due to self-doubt or procrastination. If you feel something's (or some*one*'s) been undermining you, try to find the source of that issue so that you can realize the fruits of your labor in time.

4 of Pentacles

The 4 of Pentacles signifies a foundation being built in material possessions or wealth. Your hard work is certainly paying off, and you may be well on your way to building an empire from that work. However, make sure you don't become too detached from people and emotions with all this focus on finances and work!

In reverse, this card signifies that it's finally time to open up and release the emotional burdens you've been holding on to for so long. You may have been making a storehouse of "unproductive" emotions, and now is the perfect time to face that storehouse head on, so you can heal and actually move forward.

5 of Pentacles

The 5 of Pentacles represents financial bereavements. Unexpected loss recently slapped you in the face (or it soon will!), so you're feeling undermined, underwhelmed, disappointed, and disillusioned. Don't let this pain break you down completely, for material goods can be regained. Re-examine your life to see what other types of abundance you may have been overlooking in order to heal this wound.

In reverse, this card signifies a turning point of sorts. It may not be financial, and it's more than likely relationship-based instead. This turning point has been signaled to you through your intense desire to recreate failed emotional intimacies with new people. Allow these new (relationship) foundations to be structured from the ruins of what others have left behind. Transform that negativity into something more productive!

6 of Pentacles

The 6 of Pentacles symbolizes that you can't receive abundance in a vacuum—you have to put goodness and abundance out into the world in order to receive it for yourself. This card, therefore, encourages individuals to channel generosity with others as much as possible. The more selfless you can become, the more the universe will be able to recognize your goodness, and then it will provide for you in kind.

In reverse, this card signifies struggles with money as well as debt to others. You may be working through selfishness–or you may be attempting more caution– when it comes to money. Anything you can do to become selfless and generous will help you cure this imbalance. And once the imbalance is cured, the universe will send blessings your way too.

7 of Pentacles

The 7 of Pentacles reveals that it's time to harvest the fruits of your relationships! Whether professional, personal, or romantic, your relationships will be especially abundant at this point, and you'll likely learn a good number of lessons in terms of relating to others at this time. Don't worry about interfering with things in your life in order to affirm any future growth, for it will happen to you without any effort on your part. You are aligned with success, and the only thing you can do to help is to clean out any (emotional, physical, or spiritual) clutter that remains.

In reverse, this card signifies that your life, your work, and/or your relationships are not currently satisfying. They're not only dissatisfying; they're also energetically *frustrating*. If you feel things are unfair or unequal in these realms right now, don't let patience or exhaustion stand in the way of you expressing your truth.

8 of Pentacles

The 8 of Pentacles is a card focused on patience. This card recognizes that you currently have huge goals and that you've been putting in a lot of hard work. It sees your successes and hardships, and it wants you to succeed even further, but just know that this outcome will require even *more* hard work. Work like a turtle (slow and steady) until your end-goals are settled firmly in sight! It could be that you're about to enter an internship or apprenticeship that realigns your direction entirely, too.

In reverse, this card signifies that you're hoping for success without any work to support these hopes. You've got grand dreams, but you're physically lazy. There's a disjunction–an imbalance–between theory and application, and you won't truly become established and prolific until you correct these imbalances. You might be in the wrong vocational field entirely, as a matter of fact!

9 of Pentacles

The 9 of Pentacles represents all that success will establish in your life once you have it. You will experience an abundance of all sorts, and you will have new pleasures to experience with others you trust. Furthermore, this card suggests that you will only be able to establish that success once your environment matches your values. It could be that a change of vocation is in order, so that you can work in alignment with your ethics.

In reverse, this card signifies that you are lost from the path you worked so hard to find. It could be that you haven't found your path at all, and the weight of that truth weighs on you. It could be, on the other hand, that you're unable to accept the responsibility necessary to succeed in this manner. Relocate your priorities, and get back in touch with discipline to balance out this issue.

10 of Pentacles

The 10 of Pentacles focuses on what's called an attitude of gratitude, or a mindset of abundance. When you pull the 10 of Pentacles, your higher self is telling you to wake up and realize your blessings! There are likely far more than you've recently noticed. Feel the weight of these blessings in your life, express gratitude often, and accept that your mindset attracts abundance. If you're working to attract abundance of this nature without success, don't fret. This card reminds you that outcomes are sometimes delayed in order to teach a message. For you, this time the message is likely: be patient.

In reverse, this card signifies that the bonds of family are either troubling or unproductive to you at the current moment. It may help you to see a distinction between "Earth family" and "chosen family." Embrace your friends, your pets, and your close colleagues as kin, and allow yourself to detach from and release the pressures put on you by any troubling Earth family members. You owe them nothing, especially if they don't appreciate you.

Page of Pentacles

The Page of Pentacles insists that a new (and profitable!) phase of your life is about to begin. Especially at this time, take note of any ideas that enter your head! They are likely to be the intellectual seeds of your future business or other high-achieving projects.

In reverse, this card signifies that you've been working too hard for something that's just an idea (at this point, at least). Don't overextend yourself for a project that's far from completion. Work some, plan some, and relax some! That last step is crucial for your mental and physical health.

Knight of Pentacles

The Knight of Pentacles represents a practical and supportive person (or approach) that's about to impact your life intensely. Your goals for the immediate future likely involve getting back in touch with health through a new (or new-to-you) dietary or fitness practice. This card can also mean that a journey over land will be undertaken soon.

In reverse, this card signifies a person (or attitude) that's overly focused on material abundance to the detriment of spiritual, emotional, and mental practices of betterment. Don't forget to focus on healing and affirming your whole self, rather than just parts of yourself! Furthermore, this card can represent inner turmoil being turned into positivity in a variety of ways.

Queen of Pentacles

The Queen of Pentacles represents a person (or attitude) that needs to devote more care to one's body, one's land, one's possessions, one's financial estate, and/or one's relationships. This question asks the querent what he or she is doing to support the land we come from. Furthermore, this card can represent the need to treat yourself if times have been hard.

In reverse, this card signifies an unfortunate internal state during which you may not recognize, trust, or support yourself, your instincts, and your dreams. Get back outside and in touch with nature if you're feeling this disassociation occurring. You can also recalibrate these feelings about yourself by getting back in touch with your animal self. Let go of what you're hoarding and donate material goods that don't serve you. Skim down on *things* to find yourself again.

King of Pentacles

The King of Pentacles is all about seeking (and achieving) improvement to one's financial situation. You've been working long and hard, and those efforts are about to pay off if they haven't already. Your own potential for traditional success (artistically or professionally) lies right under your nose.

In reverse, this card signifies the worst that high-achieving earthy energy has to offer. Essentially, it suggests stubbornness, rigidity, disrespectfulness, condescension, vulgarity, jealousy, and general inadequacy (pridefully posing as success). Keep an eye out for this problematic energy in your life.

Memorization Tricks

This section devotes its focus to establishing and explaining 5 different tricks you can use make memorizing all the meanings in the tarot a little easier. There are hidden patterns and meanings in the deck that you only need to know so that things will be immensely simpler. Check in with the tricks below to learn more!

Trick #1 – The Story in the Major Arcana

If you're having a hard time remembering the order of the Major Arcana, this trick may help you a lot. Similarly, if you're struggling to remember the *meanings* of the Major Arcana cards, this trick will be equally helpful. There is a story about the history of humanity that's told in these first 22 cards, and once you know that story and its progressions, you may have a much easier time with your understanding of your own deck. The story follows this basic path: At first, humankind emerged from the UNKNOWN (The Fool, #0). Then, these bumbling humans realized the strength of their WILL (The Magician, #1) to change their circumstances, the importance of INTUITION (The High Priestess, #2) to tell what's true, the value of CREATIVITY (The Empress, #3) to populate the world, and the trickiness of REASON (The Emperor, #4), being that it's so important yet so hard to fully attain. TRADITION (The Hierophant, #5) taught these humans what had value, but CHOICE (The Lover, #6) gave them the ability to select what they wanted for themselves. Humans rose up TRIUMPHANT (The Chariot, #7) with their freedoms and felt DETERMINED (Strength, #8) to take on the ever-expanding world. However, with all these successes, humanity became INTROSPECTIVE (The Hermit, #9) regarding all those choices and paths not taken. Humanity felt the true weight of all the passing CHANGES (The Wheel of Fortune, #10) in their surrounding world and felt the need for true BALANCE (Justice, #11). With this urge for balance, however, there was a need for SACRIFICE (The Hanged Man, #12) and ENDINGS (Death, #13) of what no longer served the population. In the end, a BLENDING (Temperance, #14) of cultures and temperaments was achieved to the benefit of all. MATERIAL THINGS (The Devil, #15) increased, along with their destructive forces, while our DEEP INSIGHTS (The Tower, #16) into those losses were often ignored. Still, some humans had HOPE (The Star, #17), while others were stuck in the same DELUSIONS and ILLUSIONS (The Moon, #18) that things didn't need to change anymore. Eventually, the truth was ILLUMINATED (The Sun, #19) for all to see, and great AWAKENINGS (Judgment, #20) spread across the land. Spirituality woke up in the population, giving them the truest GIFT (The World, #21) of existence. Ultimately, new humans were born with fresh INNOCENCE (The Fool, #22), despite their ancestors' wrongs, continuing this cycle into the future.

Trick #2 – The Elements in the Suits

A great trick for remembering the meaning of each suit in the Minor Arcana is to associate a natural element with each one. Wands are associated with fire, Cups are linked with water, Pentacles signify earth, and Swords are tied to air. Elementally, that means that Wands are linked with initiatory energy, adventure, travel, passions, and action, so any wand card you draw will have this energy deeply infused into it. Cups are linked with emotionality, deep feeling, introspection, healing, and curiosity, so any Cups you pull will have this associated energy. Pentacles are therefore associated with groundedness, home life, domesticity, earthwork, gardening, material goods, and financial prospects, so any Pentacles you draw will have this essential energy. Finally, Swords are linked with intellectual exploration, mental capacities, socialness, educational development, and the mind itself, so any Swords you draw in a reading will relate to this type of focus.

Trick #3 – The Meaning in the Numbers

While this association will be explained fully in Chapter 6, for now, it will suffice to say that the numbers on each card mean more than just their successive order in the series. Numbers contain intense power and significance, and if you can understand what the numbers on each card signify, you will have a much easier time memorizing both the Major and Minor Arcana.

Trick #4 – The Court / Face Cards

Within the Minor Arcana, 16-20 cards can be worked with individually in order for an easier time with memorization. These cards are the Court or Face cards. Often called Page, Knight, Queen, King, (and Ace) these cards *can* have different names, such as Princess, Prince, etc. Consult your deck for more specifics to see what the author decided to call them.

Essentially, each of these face cards represents a different phase of the individual's self-expression. While the Major

Arcana discuss the inner mysteries of humanity as a whole and its journey across time to today, the Minor Arcana talks more about individual people, traits, and experiences that come to shape each person's self-expression in this lifetime.

Whenever you see a Page, know that the energy is focused on inexperienced energy that aches for self-expression. Pages in Cups and Pentacles represent feminine energy of the goddess, slowness, and receptivity, while Pages in Swords and Wands represent masculine energy of the god, activity, and projection. This inexperienced energy is also idealistic and innocent, regardless of its gendered association.

Whenever you see a Knight, know that the energy is focused on immature energy that aches for knowledge and teachings. Knights in Cups and Pentacles are feminine, while Swords and Wands are masculine, as with Pages. This immature energy of the Knight is also charming and hopeful in its approach, regardless of its gendered association.

Whenever you see a Queen, know that the energy is focused on increased maturity and actualization of goals. As with Pages and Knights, Queens are divided between feminine (Cups and Pentacles) and masculine (Swords and Wands), which affects the energetic interpretation of the card. For example, a Queen of Swords represents actualization of intellectual goals, while the Queen of Wands represents actualization of physical or passionate goals.

Whenever you see a King, know that the energy is focused on responsibility, knowledge, cynicism, and disillusionment. As with the rest of the face cards, there are different gendered associations for Kings based on their suit-type. Ultimately, Kings suggest that what one desired wasn't as fulfilling as one hoped, hence the responsibility *alongside* the disillusionment.

Finally, whenever you see an Ace, know that the energy is focused on new beginnings and hunches for new action. Just like the other suited cards, each suit has a gendered association that affects *where* in one's life he or she will feel or notice these new beginnings. That about sums it up! For your convenience, there is an exercise included in Chapter 5 that will help you to practice this helpful memorization trick!

Trick #5 – Read a Lot!

This memorization trick isn't necessarily the easiest of the bunch, but it will surely be helpful! The gist is to get your hands on as many books about tarot as you can. If you can, get your hands on different types of decks too! Read about the cards' meanings, the imagery, and the way the author talks about memorizing the meanings. Read as much as you can, and the more tarot books you can access, the quicker you'll be able to understand what they mean (and how they all work together).

Chapter 4: The Spreads

Now that you've chosen your deck and have a basic understanding of each card– either in your working memory or to draw upon later in these pages–you are ready for the fun part: doing your own tarot readings! This chapter comes equipped with 20 different spreads so that you can practice with your cards, and each spread has a specific theme or intention. You'll find spreads for introspection and awareness, for each sign in the Western zodiac, for self-diagnosis of illness, and so much more!

Before you do any spread or tarot reading, make sure to cleanse your deck (if it's being used for someone else or if someone else touched your deck recently for any reason), shuffle it well, and put yourself in the moment with all thoughts on what you will ask of the deck.

In order to cleanse your deck, if necessary, the best technique is to use smoke. Light a stick of incense and run your cards through the smoke or apply the same technique with the smoke of burned sage bundles or other dried herbal bundles, incenses, or resins. You can also cleanse your deck with crystals by either making a crystal grid around your deck or by setting a powerful cleansing stone (like Amethyst or Clear Quartz) on top of your deck while you wait. Just about a minute in the smoke or with the crystals should do the trick!

Then, shuffle the deck gently while you calm your mind and think of the question you'll be asking.

1. Spread for Past, Present, Future

For this tarot reading, you will focus on where you've come from (your past), where you are now (your present), and where you're about to go (your future). You only need to pull 3 cards, so after you've cleansed and shuffled your deck, think about those three elements: your past, your present, and your future. Think about what you've struggled through and where you hope to be. Lay the three cards face-down first, and arrange them any way you like, but make sure the first represents your past, the second represents your present, and the third represents your future. Flip all three over at once or one at a time to divine your answers.

2. Spread to Identify Three Aspects of the Self

Just like the last spread, you're going to pull only 3 cards, but unlike the last spread, you're going to think about yourself as a whole being rather than about moments in time in your life. After you've cleansed and shuffled the deck, therefore, ask the cards to provide you a glimpse at, for example, your 3 strongest traits, your 3 biggest weaknesses, your 3 biggest lessons for this lifetime, your 3 best job possibilities, or any other 3 major aspects of yourself. As with the first spread, feel free to flip all cards over at once or to interpret one at a time.

3. Spread of Self-Identification (The Grand, or Celtic, Cross)

This spread takes a few more cards to complete than the previous two. You'll need to pull 10 cards for this reading, and you can honestly lay them out any way you like, but the general idea is to make a cross shape with your cards. You can find exact replicas of this spread online if you'd like a picture for assistance, but I'll try to explain it as simply as possible, so you won't have to look elsewhere. Start as usual: cleanse and shuffle your deck. As you're shuffling, choose a question to focus on about yourself or your life.

Lay down your first card in the middle of the space in front of you. Card 1 will represent yourself and your general relationship to the question you're asking. Card 2 will be laid overtop card 1 but sideways, making a cross over that first card, and card 2 will represent any obstacles that directly stand in the way of your path.

Card 3 goes to the left of card 1, and it will represent what is behind you, what you've worked through, and what you can now use to your advantage. Card 4 goes on the other side of card 1, to the right side. It will represent what's generally ahead for you, and what you may need to look out for.

Card 5 goes below card 1, and it suggests something you've grown out of, something that's beneath you that you had to learn from to evolve. Card 6 goes above card 1, and it talks about the best qualities of yourself and the way you access your higher self. Now, by looking at these first 6 cards, you should have that basic cross shape established! Feel free to flip over these cards now and process their meaning in terms of your question.

The next four cards go one after the other in a vertical line next to your cross on its right side. Starting at the bottom, lay card 7, which will represent how you're feeling about moving forward with this new knowledge. Then above card 7, lay card 8, which will demonstrate what the attitudes of people around you are in relation to this matter.

Above card 8 goes card 9, which talks about your greatest fears and hopes in terms of moving forward with this knowledge. Finally, card 10 goes above card 9, and it suggests literally what is to come next, whether that means an experience, a life change, a person, or otherwise. Flip over these four cards now and interpret their meaning alone as well as in reference to the original 6 cards. You'll surely have some questions answered about yourself with this spread!

4. Spread for Aries

This spread will work best for both readers and querents who are Aries (sun sign or ascending/rising sign), so if you're the not an Aries but you're reading the cards for someone who *is*, this might be a great spread to start with! If you *are* an Aries, try this reading out for yourself to see what you can discover!

For this reading, you'll need to pull 7 cards, and you can lay them out any way you like, but make sure you remember the order! Additionally, you don't necessarily have to ask a question in association with this spread, for you can simply learn from the cards as they fall. But if a question lays heavy on your heart as an Aries, it will certainly find some resolution through this reading, too.

Card 1 will represent how you're doing physically. Card 2 will demonstrate how your overall energy level is, and card 3 asks how you're doing in terms of control. Are you uncontrolled? Or are you reigned in and focused on succeeding? Card 3 will have something to say about that.

Card 4 talks about how your excitement is for life, and how enthusiastic you're feeling. Card 5 asks what you're running away from in life, Aries. Card 6 shows you how to best approach your goals and dreams, and card 7 reveals what those deepest, truest goals and dreams really are. Lay down your cards one at a time and process them individually for the best results.

5. Spread for Taurus

Similarly, for the Aries spread, this one works best for Taurus readers and querents, so be aware! This Taurus reading requires 7 cards, and they can also be laid out any way the reader wants. Again, you don't really need to ask a question with this spread, for it will provide good advice and direction for Taurus regardless.

Card 1 asks Taurus to dig deep and investigate what his or her opinions and stances on money and possessions are right now. Card 2 looks at the state of your current finances, and card 3 peers a little deeper by examining what skills and talents you're using to make this income.

Card 4 wonders whether Taurus has been feeling sexual pleasure recently (and if so, how the experiences were). Card 5 looks at how Taurus relates to luxury and excess, while card 6 questions how patient Taurus has been able to be lately. Finally, card 7 examines jealousy and possessiveness outside material goods. Ideally, this card will show where Taurus's biggest struggles currently lie. As with the Aries spread, lay down each card one at a time, and process each one before moving forward.

6. Spread for Gemini

Along the same lines as the previous two spreads, this one will work best for readers and querents who are Gemini (sun sign or ascending), and you will have to pull 8 cards for this reading. As with the other astrological readings, you can lay out your cards any way you like, and it's best to lay them out one at a time and process them individually. (Again, you don't really need to ask a question with this spread, for it will provide good advice and direction for Gemini regardless.)

Card 1 for Gemini's spread talks about how your mind is working right now. Card 2 checks on your truth and wonders how well you can lie at the moment, and card 3 wonders what (or who) you might be researching or watching presently.

Card 4 talks about family and checks in with how things are going for you with your parents and siblings. Card 5 looks at communication: how are things going? Do you fight more than you agree? Do you communicate pleasantly or aggressively? What happens when you *do* get into a fight? Consider these questions for card 5.

Card 6 discusses doubt for Gemini. What's holding you back with the power of doubt? Card 7 wonders if you're being delusional or too dreamy about anything in your life, and card 8 is the kicker for Gemini, the sign of the twins: how is your relationship with your inner twin, and what is your inner twin like?

7. Spread for Cancer

For any Cancers out there, it's time for your spread, and you'll want to pull 8 cards for this reading. Again you can arrange them any way you like but be sure to process them one at a time. (You don't really need to ask a question with this spread, for it will provide good advice and direction for Cancer regardless.)

Card 1 tells Cancer where he or she comes from, as in what family circumstances birthed this person and what complexities may have helped shape him or her. Card 2 asks you what your dreams are, Cancer! Card 3 wonders how your current home life is, and card 4 specifically questions how you view your father.

Card 5 shows you how much you *need* a security net to feel happy and safe in the world, and card 6 asks you how (or how intensely) you express your deepest feelings. Card 7 talks about your compassion: how kind and considerate are you, really? And finally, card 8 questions how psychic you are (or will be) and how awakened and advanced your abilities are right now.

8. Spread for Leo

This spread for Leos works like the other astrological readings in that it's best for Leo readers and querents. You'll pull 7 cards for this spread, and you can arrange them any way you like, but be sure to process them one at a time. (Again, you don't really need to ask a question with this spread, for it will provide good advice and direction for Leo regardless.)

Card 1 questions how intense and dominating your ego is right now, Leo. Card 2 sees the world as a stage and wonders what part of that stage you're acting on these days. Card 3 looks within you for your inner child, to see if he or she is there and how healthy that "child" is today. Card 4 wonders about your love life: how are things going and how are you feeling about love and romance right now?

Card 5 examines your admiration, respect, and compassion for children, and card 6 looks at where you take risks and relish in risky freedoms. Finally, card 7 looks to your Leonine mane. While you may be king or queen of the jungle, are you a generous ruler or a wicked one?

9. Spread for Virgo

This spread for Virgos works like the other astrological readings in that it's best for Virgo readers and querents. You'll pull 8 cards for this spread, and you can arrange them any way you like, but be sure to process them one at a time. (Again, you don't really need to ask a question with this spread, for it will provide good advice and direction for Virgo regardless).

When you pull card 1 for Virgo, it will reveal pieces of how you feel about your body as an aspect of yourself. Card 2 will reveal how interested you are in healing or medical studies.

Card 3 talks about your physical health at this moment, and card 4 questions how you're feeling about work.

Card 5 wonders how your analytical mind is working and whether you're being too critical. Card 6 looks at how easily you adjust after hardship, and card 7 reveals how consistent you are and whether you're a hypocrite. This card will show you if you're being too much of a perfectionist, too. Finally, card 8 wonders how distanced you are from life because of being too wary.

10. Spread for Libra

This spread for Libras works like the other astrological readings in that it's best for Libra readers and querents. You'll pull 9 cards for this spread, and you can arrange them any way you like, but be sure to process them one at a time. (Again, you don't really need to ask a question with this spread, for it will provide good advice and direction for Libra regardless.)

Libra's first card will talk about decision making, since Libras stereotypically have a hard time making decisions. Card 2 shows how you form relationships with others and how you socially bond. Card 3 looks at how you bond with others in a professional or vocational setting, and card 4 is more about where in your life you (strive to) fight for peace.

Card 5 reveals your potential for forgiveness or vengeance and which of the two is more familiar to you. Card 6 looks at your intimate relationships and wonders what you give away of yourself to these lovers. Card 7 encourages you to see how you might be repressing or suppressing some of your feelings, and card 8 interprets how artistic your feelings can be. Finally, card 9 looks to your worst traits: how do you act (or appear) phony and sullen?

11. Spread for Scorpio

This spread for Scorpios works like the other astrological readings in that it's best for Scorpio readers and querents. You'll pull 8 cards for this spread, and you can arrange them any way you like, but be sure to process them one at a time. (Again, you don't really need to ask a question with this spread, for it will provide good advice and direction for Scorpio regardless.)

The first card for Scorpios relates to card 7 from the Libra spread: what are you emotionally suppressing, and what tends to get suppressed more than anything else? Card 2 forces you to face your taboos, and card 3 encourages you to embrace your true sexuality. Card 4 shows you how you conceptualize your own death, and card 5 reveals your innermost values (in case you didn't already name them).

Card 6 shows what potential legacies and birthrights will be yours, and card 7 gets personal by forcing you to face your own tendency (or tendencies) for self-destruction. Finally, card 8 likens you to water, like the element of Scorpio itself: are you a creek, a lake, a river, or an ocean? In other words, how deep are you and what is your capacity for (spiritual, emotional, and intellectual) intensity in this life?

12. Spread for Sagittarius

This spread for Sagittarius works like the other astrological readings in that it's best for Sagittarius readers and querents. You'll pull 6 cards for this spread, and you can arrange them any way you like, but be sure to process them one at a time. (Again, you don't really need to ask a question with this spread, for it will provide good advice and direction for Sagittarius regardless.)

The first card for Sagittarius represents how you're interacting with your social sphere. What role do you play in these environments? Card 2 examines how your education has been up until now, and card 3 looks to your most firmly-held beliefs or practices of religion. Card 4 reveals the extent (or impact) of journeying and adventuring you've done in the outside world, while card 5 does the same for any journeying and travelling you may have done (or that you may be doing now) in reference to your own inner world. Finally, card 6 shows where you are on your life-long search for meaning and purpose (as well as what you can expect from the near future!).

13. Spread for Capricorn

This spread for Capricorns works like the other astrological readings in that it's best for Capricorn readers and querents. You'll pull 7 cards for this spread, and you can arrange them any way you like, but be sure to process them one at a time. (Again, you don't really need to ask a question with this spread, for it will provide good advice and direction for Capricorn regardless.)

Card 1 for Capricorns looks at how you feel about your career and what hopes you sense for that vocational future. Card 2 reveals how intense your wishes for power and fame are, while card 3 looks at how you are as an individual: are you as intense as your wishes for power, are you serious, and are you responsible?

Card 4 shows how your values line up with the values of the world as a whole, and card 5 examines your relationship with your mother in this lifetime. Card 6 highlights what you should aim for, as far as your goals and successes in this world. Finally, card 7 reveals what you're aiming toward with all this hard work, thoughtfulness, and dedication.

14. Spread for Aquarius

This spread for Aquarius works like the other astrological readings in that it's best for Aquarius readers and querents. You'll pull 8 cards for this spread, and you can arrange them any way you like, but be sure to process them one at a time. (Again, you don't really need to ask a question with this spread, for it will provide good advice and direction for Aquarius regardless.)

For Aquarius, your first card will demonstrate the closest friends in your life right now and what they represent for you. Card 2 shows you how you're feeling about freedom and whether you're trapped in any aspect of your life right now. Card 3 points to your role in the group: are you a leader, a worker, a follower, or what? Card 4 is all about opposition: what do you work against in the current society you inhabit? What revolutionary urges do you hold deeply?

Card 5 reveals how impulsive you can be, and card 6 looks at whether you're feeling worthy, superior, or inferior to others in this lifetime. Card 7 asks whether you're underestimating yourself or if you've got an inflated sense of self instead, and finally, card 8 shows you the path you must follow to be able to live out your dreams and follow your stars.

15. Spread for Pisces

This spread for Pisces works like the other astrological readings in that it's best for Pisces readers and querents. You'll pull 7 cards for this spread, and you can arrange them any way you like, but be sure to process them one at a time. (Again, you don't really need to ask a question with this spread, for it will provide good advice and direction for Pisces regardless.)

Pisces' first card wonders how idealistic and optimistic you are, or–the converse–how pessimistic or realistic you tend to be instead. Card 2 cuts to the core and reveals your tendency for self-sacrifice or martyrdom (either intellectually or emotionally). Card 3 shows the spiritual path you've been on and where it may lead you.

Pisces is the escapist of the Western zodiac, and the reading will keep things real by demonstrating what you're addicted to in this life with card 4. Card 5 reveals any hidden adversaries that may be creeping into your life, while card 6 points out where you may be metaphorically imprisoned or stuck. Finally, card 7 draws out the path that will save you from these setbacks and what you have to look forward to once you're liberated.

16. Spread for Self-Diagnosis of Dis-ease

For this tarot reading, we'll move away from astrological themes and towards health. This spread intends to explain, decipher, and locate the source of your internal or external dis-ease. You'll pull 5 cards for this spread, and it's ideal that you sit on the ground to do this reading because you'll arrange those 5 cards around you like five points of a star with you at the center.

Card 1 will be placed directly in front of you, and it signifies the source of your power, how you gain energy, and how your body then uses that energy. Card 2 will be placed to your right as the second point on the star, and it represents what you're currently feeling inside, in terms of dis-ease. Card 3 will be placed to your right and slightly behind you as the third point on the star. It suggests where that dis-ease might spiritually or emotionally come from.

Card 4 will be placed to your left and slightly behind you, and it represents what influences of others or what past life struggles may be making this dis-ease more pronounced for you right now. Finally, card 5 will be placed to your left as the final point of the star. This card signifies how you can turn things around and how you can begin to approach self-directed healing for this dis-ease.

17. Spread for the New Year

This simple 12-card spread can be used for any culture's New Year celebration, as long as the culture in question still relies on a 12-month calendar! You'll pull 1 card for each month, and you can lay them all face down before turning them over one at a time to process. While you shuffle the deck after cleansing, you can either let the cards generally predict major themes of the year ahead, or you can always infuse your reading with a particular theme or question that you'd like answered.

18. Spread for Your Birthday!

For your birthday this year, do a tarot spread for what's coming! It's absolutely simple, and you can pull any number of cards that you'd like. My go-to birthday reading is to do a 3-card pull, with the first card representing the past year that I leave behind, the second card signifying what I bring to the next year, and the third card suggesting how the next year will allow me to grow. You could also do a 12-card spread for each month of the upcoming year (like the previous New Year spread), a 4- or 5-card spread for each week in your birthday month, a 7-card spread for each day of your birthday week, or a 1-card pull for the biggest lesson you'll have to face this year.

19. Spread of the Pyramid (Facets of the Self)

This 6-card spread demonstrates 6 different sides of the self, and each card will be laid out to form the overall shape of a pyramid. Ancient Egyptians believed that there were numerous facets of the self, some of which we freely share with others and some of which we keep hidden. Therefore, there will be some sides of the self that become revealed in this tarot reading that you'll struggle to face, but once you do, you'll be able to grow in ways you may have never considered for yourself.

When you pull card 1, imagine that you're starting to build the base of your pyramid. You can leave it on its back and wait until you "build" your entire card pyramid, or you can turn it over immediately to see the side of the self that you're proud of, what you've grown consciously and are eager to share with others. Card 2 will go to the right of card 1, and it will represent the side of the self you're ashamed of and what you keep hidden at all costs. Card 3 goes to the right of card 2 and suggests the side of you that will sacrifice anything for others, the martyr side.

Card 4 will establish the second row of the pyramid, so put it above cards 1 and 2, yet right in between them. This card demonstrates the side of yourself that's a scholar, a lover of knowledge. For what area of study do you feel this love, and what do you do when you feel it? Card 5 goes to the right of card 4, and it should be above and between cards 2 and 3. This card signifies the side of the self that is a lover. How do you love, who do you love, and how can you share that with the world? Finally, card 6 will make the top of the pyramid in a row above cards 4 and 5 but right between them. This card represents the final aspect of your pyramid, which is how you bring all these other facets together and fuse them into your identity and self-expression.

20. Spread for the Week Ahead

Similar to the New Year spread, which requires a card for each month in the year, this reading for the week ahead requires as many cards as there are days in the week. Once you've pulled those 7 cards, arrange them any way you like, and overturn them individually or all at once. Whether you start your mental calendar on Monday or Sunday, the first card you lay down may vary, so go by what feels right to you. For me, card 1 is Sunday, card 2 is Monday, card 3 is Tuesday, etc. This reading will give you a great sense of what to expect from the week ahead whenever you need a psychic boost!

While some of these tarot spreads are more complicated or involved than others, they all demonstrate a very good place to start. They're accessible, they're easy to understand, they're insightful, and they're going to be extremely helpful in both your life as a whole and your growing relationship with the tarot. You can find any number of additional spreads in other books and online, but you can also invent your own tarot readings as you go! Try these for a start, then unleash the floodgates! There's so much to be explored.

Chapter 5: Exercises & Brain Boosters

If you're still looking for more to do with the tarot aside from simply looking at the cards to learn them or trying readings out on yourself, fear not! You haven't reached the end of the road with tarot, for there's so much more you can do. This chapter provides 10 exercises with the cards that you can play around with in order to better understand what tarot is all about.

There is a difficulty rating included in the explanation of each exercise so that you will know what you're getting yourself into. The rating uses a simple scale of 1 to 3, with 1 being super easy, 2 being average difficulty, and 3 being more complicated. Additionally, before this chapter ends, you'll receive 3 tips to use as brain boosters with your overall tarot experience. There's a lot to learn, so dive right in!

Exercise #1 – Find Your Tarot Card for the Year

This exercise will take you deeper into the meaning of one card each year, and the card linked with you will become incredibly symbolic for your next 12 months. On the turn of the New Year, as the year number ticks up to one more, you can figure out your tarot Growth Card for the year ahead. All you have to do is add the day and month of your birthday with the digits of the new year. For example, say your birthday is 5/25/1961, and it just became 2019. You'd add 5 (the month) + 2 + 5 (the day) to get 12 and then add 12 + 2 + 0 + 1 + 9 to get your ending number of 24.

Then, you'd associate this number with its corresponding card in the Major Arcana. However, there are only 22 cards in the Major Arcana, so if you get to a number greater than 22 (like this example's 24), you'd add the individual digits of the number to find which card links with you instead. For example, 24 becomes 2 + 4, which is 6, so the corresponding Major Arcana card for this person in this New Year would be the Lovers. By looking at this card closely for its symbolism and by analyzing all its potential meanings, this person will discover what the upcoming year has in store for him or her.

Difficulty level: 1

Exercise #2 – Gather a Few Decks Together

This exercise is designed to help you understand the symbolism behind the cards rather than just the information, meanings, and words packed within them. I can explain what each card means until the cows come home, but sometimes that just doesn't stick. Instead, you can get visual with your deck! And if you have multiple decks, combine them and see what the different artists were thinking about, say, the Moon card or the Strength card.

This type of close looking is a great way to perceive the messages behind the images, for there are so many images and symbols within the pictures of each card that can allow you to understand their meanings better than any book of descriptions could. Essentially, if you can, gather together a few decks and look to the imagery in the pictures. Take notes if you want, but even just by looking, you will expand your appreciation of the cards greatly.

Difficulty level: 2 (simply due to the cost of acquiring several decks)

Exercise #3 – Pull a Daily Card

To become more familiar with your deck in particular (as well as the cards in general), you are absolutely invited to start pulling a daily card! This practice is extremely effective to help newcomers to tarot become more understanding of what their decks (and the tarot overall) can offer. It's up to you whether you pull your card in the morning, in mid-day, or the evening after everything's already happened, but the point is to draw a card each day so that you're constantly practicing with the deck while boosting your divination and psychic abilities.

For those who are actually newcomers to tarot, I always recommend starting this exercise with all the cards facing the same direction. Without the "reversed" card option in play, you can get a solid working knowledge of what the cards mean generally. Then, after a few weeks or months of pulling a card a day, when you're ready to add in the "reversed" option, please do! You'll find that waiting to add in this layer of tarot can really help for those who are either overwhelmed or confused.

Difficulty level: 1

Exercise #4 – Download a Tarot App

If you don't have your own deck yet (or if you don't want to bring your deck everywhere with you), try downloading an app for tarot on your phone or tablet! There are so many good tarot apps out there, and many of them are free. Frequently, apps of this type offer options for daily readings, bigger tarot spreads, individual card information, and sometimes even journaling based on what cards you pull.

It may seem ingenuine to approach the tarot technologically, but the same rules apply as will be explained in tip #3 later on. You're in charge, not the cards and not the app. Your higher self is who and what guides the reading and who delivers the overall meaning. So, don't knock the app option until you've tried it! You may be surprised how much it helps to have a virtual deck with you on the go everywhere. When it comes down to it, it's also just a helpful, handy, informative option! The quicker you get familiar with these cards, the better!

Difficulty level: 1

Exercise #5 – Make a Chart for Your Daily Pulls

For those who are extra studious and who love making lists, you're bound to attach to exercise 5 immediately. The goal of this exercise is to allow you to track the cards you've pulled in the past year, to note patterns, and to observe themes in your readings based on what's happened in your life. All you have to do is start a daily practice of pulling one card each day. Then, it's time to get crafty.

You'll want to make a big chart with maybe 10 columns going across the top, and every card of the tarot deck making rows going down the side. Based on the card you pull each day, you'll mark it on the chart which one it was, and then after a month, a few months, or a year, you will see how frequently you've pulled each card as well as which ones you may have somehow avoided. Based on these frequencies and accidental avoidances, you'll find which themes have played out in the past month, months, or year, and you can enhance your overall understanding of the cards, too.

Difficulty level: 3 (requires focus & consistency over time as well as creativity)

Exercise #6 – What Does the Card Want You to Know?

This exercise is kind of like doing a tarot reading in reverse. Often, you know what you will be laying out, how many cards there will be, and what each card will symbolize. However, this exercise turns that method on its head and thereby helps you access your connection to your higher self (and to the cards) better. Ultimately, you'll still cleanse, shuffle, and vibe with the deck as usual. You can still ask the deck an overall question or feel a certain energy when you shuffle, hoping for answers and resolutions. The trick is that you won't know what you're pulling for until you pull the card.

You'll want to be very open, centered, and grounded when you attempt this exercise because it is a little more difficult. You also want to be so open and grounded because you're going to have to dig deeper with yourself and the cards this time after asking your question. When you pull each card, sit with it for a few moments before flipping it over so that you can let your higher self tell you which aspect of your question this card refers to.

You can pull as many cards as needed, and I recommend trying to take note of what they signify as soon as you pick up on that information from your higher self. That way, when you finally flip the cards over, you'll still remember what each one relates to in reference to your overall question. At that point, you can conduct your reading, as usual, to see how your question has been answered.

Difficulty level: 3 (requires hefty intuition & psychic focus)

Exercise #7 – Find a Tarot "Study Buddy"

It might not seem imminently helpful, but another person getting interested in tarot with you can mean all the difference for some beginning practitioners! Group work can be incredibly beneficial in reference to tarot because the people in the group become accountable to one another, and fierce study of the cards can be instigated. Furthermore, working with at least one other person can keep the information fresh, enabling you to understand more about the tarot even faster. I hope that you will end up doing readings for one another to put the knowledge into practice!

Difficulty level: 2

Exercise #8 – Associate Your Own Keywords for Each Card

This exercise is for those more studious individuals who want to understand their cards' meanings quickly with no dilly-dallying! The gist of the exercise is to go through all the cards in the deck, and in a journal or notebook somewhere, take note of 2-4 keywords that describe each one. Eventually, you may be able to use your notebook of keywords when you're conducting your readings more than you use the information provided in this book! Regardless of how you use it, putting this massive store of information into your own words and then writing all that down allows your brain to process every piece of knowledge better and more holistically.

For those who are increasingly studious and looking for even more work, I recommend doing the same exercise for the "reversed" meanings of the cards as well. On the other hand, you could always write 2 keywords for the standard card placement and 2 more keywords for the "reversed" placement right away in the same journal! However, you choose to do it, this exercise will absolutely help you understand your deck better, and it will give you a powerful psychic and confidence boost for all your future readings.

Difficulty level: 2 (requires a fair amount of effort)

Exercise #9 – Try it with Court Cards Only

Sometimes, people are just overwhelmed with the entire tarot deck, so I'll recommend an exercise based on slimming things down. Essentially, you can take out any segment of the tarot deck and use that for your reading instead of the entire deck. I like to choose related segments of the deck for exercises of this type. For example, this exercise in particular recommends you try a few readings using only the court (or face) cards in the Minor Arcana.

There are 56 cards in the Minor Arcana compared to the 22 of the Major Arcana, so even just working with the entire Minor segment can be a lot for an overwhelmed practitioner.

Slim things down even further by pulling out all the Aces, Pages, Knights, Queens, and Kings of each set and using just them for a few readings. Readings of this nature are best suited for questions regarding bigger life events or queries about people in your life. You're sure to get some firm answers to your questions, but you'll also learn so much more about these 20 cards in the tarot deck than you would if they were just 20 out of 56 (or 20 out of 78).

Difficulty level: 1

Exercise #10 – Try it with Major Arcana Only

Similar to exercise 9, this exercise focuses on reading one's fortune using only the 22 Major Arcana cards. These cards demonstrate the major events in one's lifetime, so questions best suited for this type of reading are ones relating to the "flavor" of one's life direction, what stage of life you're inhabiting, and what your overall goals in this lifetime should be.

Difficulty level: 1

Now to break things up in terms of these exercises, it's time to get straight to the tips! If you're feeling overwhelmed by the tarot, confused, unsure, or misdirected, touch back in with these tips, and you won't go wrong, I promise. Additionally, if you need just a little support or positive and encouraging advice, come back to these tips, too. They're sure to remind you of how powerful you (and your tarot deck) can be.

Tip #1 – Don't Overreach or Overwhelm Yourself!

If you do happen to feel overwhelmed in consideration of the tarot, try not to panic, and don't let yourself give up! These cards demonstrate powerful energetic archetypes that can teach us so much, and it would be a shame for you to give up simply because there's a lot of information! Of course, there is! Remind yourself to see the fun in that knowledge, and when you are feeling overwhelmed, try to scale things back to a more simple approach. Try a simpler reading or use exercises 9 or 10 to scale the deck back to a manageable amount of information. Process a little at a time, and you will be able to release this feeling in no time.

For those that aren't necessarily overwhelmed by the tarot but who are, perhaps, trying to do too much, consider this: you may be doing a lot *with* the cards, but do you really *know* them yet? Do you actually remember any of the spreads you've done, and are you starting to remember any particular cards? The goal is to answer these questions with a firm and resounding "yes," so if you need to re-simplify and rescale things to a more manageable amount of content (even if you feel like you don't need this step), don't be ashamed! Go ahead with the rescaling and then you'll re-emerge with confidence, knowledge, and true *ability* to handle all this overreaching from before.

Tip #2 – Keep a Tarot Journal

Anyone who reads tarot cards will benefit from keeping a tarot journal. You don't even need a physical notebook, for you can keep notes on your phone these days! Note what cards appear often, and what cards you're particularly drawn to. Note how you're feeling about your readings, how accurate they are, and how you intend to proceed with your life afterward. The more you're processing this bulk of information, the better you'll be able to integrate the learning experiences into your life, so don't be afraid to jot down things that feel important!

However works for you, start recording those tarot experiences, tarot readings, and intense card pulls. With time, you may notice patterns between the cards pulled and events in your life or emotional moments. You may also notice your psychic powers and intuition growing, and those things are equally important to take note of! Embrace the change tarot offers by keeping a record of every life-altering realization. In a few years, you'll be a tarot expert with this practice.

Tip #3 – Remember Who's in Charge!

I know it's still likely hard to imagine, but when you're doing tarot readings, you're the star. Your higher self connects with you through the archetypes in the cards, and that connection enables you to answer these questions truthfully and provide direction for your future. When you're feeling overwhelmed or frustrated by the tarot, don't let your anger with the cards get in the way! It's not their fault! You're still learning, and that's absolutely okay. Allow yourself to be patient, to be forgiven, and to be the one in charge of the experience.

If you're frustrated because you don't understand the messages the cards are telling you, try to remember that it might be *you* who's not open to receiving the messages. It's not the cards being worthless or bad quality; it's probably not even that they're wrong. When you feel this frustration, just remember that the power of tarot lies within your own soul. Open yourself to the message, and try approaching the spread again. Don't get upset with yourself, either, when things get frustrating or confusing! It's all a practice that will settle and solidify within you in time. Learning may be tough, but your future self will be so grateful you took the time.

Chapter 6: Extensions of Tarot

Tarot has intimate and innate connections with the worlds of numerology and astrology. Each card is associated with a number, and each number has a specific meaning that can help you understand the cards better. Furthermore, each card has an archetypal energy that links well with the symbols of the Western zodiac. Tarot looks at these astrological symbols and elemental energies and sees the reflection of some of its own cards and energies.

This chapter will be dedicated to hashing out these intimate and innate connections. We will first walk through the power of numerology in relation to tarot before engaging in astrological and elemental associations. I hope that by the end of this chapter, you will have a few more tricks to memorize your deck, and you will also be able to understand the power of the symbols that run through all of these powerful divination systems (including tarot reading, numerology, astrology, among so many others). You'll be an expert in reading the tarot in no time with these important informational extensions in place.

Tarot & Numerology

The 3rd memorization trick in Chapter 3 hinted that numbers have a deep meaning that often goes unacknowledged. Tarot is a great realm to finally acknowledge that truth. Furthermore, that 3rd trick suggested that by memorizing the numerological associations, remembering major themes in your deck becomes easy and so much more accessible. The details of those associations will be revealed below.

Remember that every card is associated with a number, and most decks will print the number directly on the card for your ease. The Major Arcana number from 1-22 (or 0), and the Minor Arcana go from Aces to Kings, which technically number from 0 to 14. Look to the number on the card and align it with the card's element (recall that trick #2 in Chapter 3 reveals these associations) to have a basic understanding of the entire deck without needing a book in your hands at all.

The Meaning of 0 (Zero)

Zero is said to represent all that exists as potential in the universe. 0 is the connection we share with everything else through the simple fact that we exist. We are here now, and that means we can be anything. 0 reveals that potential. 0 also demonstrates the concepts of connectedness, understanding, and wholeness.

The Meaning of 1

The Number 1 is said to represent new beginnings, taking initiatives, and finding a simple sense of completion. It is a number fulfilled in itself, and it has its own internal balance that doesn't depend on anything else. 1 demonstrates the promise of something good coming, and it also relates to one's powers of manifestation.

The Meaning of 2

The Number 2 is said to represent one's relationships with others. It signifies connectivity, intimacy, and romance as well as platonic relationships of all sorts. 2 is about interplay, interactivity, and the choice you have within all those varying options. 2 demonstrates all that experience with others has to teach you.

The Meaning of 3

The Number 3 is said to represent what happens as a product of union. 2 is about that union in many senses, but 3 reveals the creative product, result, or outcome. 3 is the essence of creativity and expression. Furthermore, it demonstrates the path of growth. 3 demonstrates the importance and value of synthesis.

The Meaning of 4

The Number 4 is said to represent stability, home life, and structure. 4 is all about what happens under 4 walls, or what becomes complete with a 4th line: the square. The square additionally symbolizes numerological perfection in some ways. 4 is a number that exists within nature too as a backbone and stabilizer, so it demonstrates this material world we inhabit.

The Meaning of 5

The Number 5 is said to represent both health and crisis in health. It is the same number as there are points on a star, which relates to the pentagram (associated with selflessness and goodness) and the pentacle (its inverse, associated with self-focus and variability). 5 is a divine number that reveals a transformation will come; however, it also demonstrates the extremes of that transformation potential.

The Meaning of 6

The Number 6 is said to represent natural harmony or balance, and it is another number that suggests a union is in order. In this case, 6 represents the divine marriage between divine masculine and divine feminine, which can take place within each individual as well as between individuals in the world. It's a number that demonstrates connection and the integrated knowledge that will emerge from it.

The Meaning of 7

The Number 7 is said to represent magic itself. 7 is the number of mysteries, the occult, the divine, and what remains hidden (although often in plain sight). This number correlates with expanded education on many levels, too, whether that occurs through self-guided study, spiritual practice, metaphorically going back to basics, or literally going back to school. In sum, 7 demonstrates what can happen when you experiment, take risks, research, and develop your own inner magic.

The Meaning of 8

The Number 8 is said to represent abundance itself. 8 is also a manifestation number that's intimately connected with the divine. In many pagan calendars, 8 holy holidays were celebrated, and 8 still represents the number of seasonal holidays we hold dear. 8 demonstrates the importance of worship and celebration, as well as all that comes from that: prosperity and the essence of abundance.

The Meaning of 9

The Number 9 is said to represent completion that aims toward leadership. You are following a cycle that's about to be completed, and that will mean new options for you. 9 signifies this energy. Furthermore, 9 demonstrates what happens when you're fully selfless and allow yourself to be directed by divinity. 9 is about the healing that can be enacted for self and others when you're openly loving.

The Meaning of 10

The Number 10 combines the energies of 1 and 0; it is said to represent new beginnings like the number 1, but it's more importantly about how endings are often new beginnings in disguise, using that essential energy of 0, too. 10 is a number of culmination and things ending. It is also a number that demonstrates freshness and transformation.

The Meaning of 11

The Number 11 combines the energies of 1 and 1; it is said to represent spiritual awakening. In the tarot, 11 associates with Pages from the Minor Arcana and with the Justice card from the Major Arcana, but the number itself represents intuition, inspiration, and connection with one's higher self. 11 demonstrates the importance of listening both to one's inner voice and to the voices of the world in order to establish ethics, morality, direction, and a sense of righteousness.

The Meaning of 12

The Number 12 combines the energies of 1 and 2; it is said to represent new beginnings based on liberation, independence, and self-reliance. In the tarot, 12 associates with Knights from the Minor Arcana and with the Hanged Man card from the Major Arcana, but the number itself represents what happens when you realize your life purpose and/or soul mission: everything fake fades away, and you become the most authentic version of yourself possible. 12 demonstrates that capability.

The Meaning of 13

The Number 13 combines the energies of 1 and 3; it is said to represent one's powers of manifestation. In the tarot, 13 associates with Queens from the Minor Arcana and with the Death card from the Major Arcana, but the number itself represents that what seems harsh may be exactly what you asked for. 13 shows you how your circumstances are more of your making than you may have realized before, yet it also demonstrates potential to break new ground with this realization.

The Meaning of 14

The Number 14 combines the energies of 1 and 4; it is said to represent a warning regarding money matters and that some test may be coming soon. In the tarot, 14 associates with Kings from the Minor Arcana and with Temperance from the Major Arcana, but the number itself represents sacrifices you may have to make if you desire to achieve your goals. It demonstrates beneficial challenges ahead that will result in lasting successes.

The Meaning of 15

The Number 15 combines the energies of 1 and 5; it is said to represent your increasing awareness that positive change is coming. You're about to realize what's been holding you back all along, and that may be painful, but you'll emerge stronger than ever. 15 reminds you to keep your eyes on the prize so that you aren't held back by the struggles that lay ahead. It demonstrates resilience, strength, needed transformation, and introspection.

The Meaning of 16

The Number 16 combines the energies of 1 and 6; it is said to represent material success to come. 16 is all about your ability to turn obstacles into positive outcomes, and the number suggests that you may find the next example of this ability sooner than you thought. 16 encourages you to have faith and stand strong, for it demonstrates how your willpower will win out after all.

The Meaning of 17

The Number 17 combines the energies of 1 and 7; it is said to represent an aspect of levelling up in your life. For the most part, 17 relates to levelled-up manifestation experience. Your intuition will be your greatest guide through this adaptation, but remember that big changes are imminent! 17 demonstrates how you'll have to step up to the plate for this levelling up to occur.

The Meaning of 18

The Number 18 combines the energies of 1 and 8; it is said to represent increased discernment, wisdom, and confidence. The outcome of such positivity will be increased capacity for abundance, which works well after 17 gave you all the manifestation experience you could need. 18 will encourage you to use all that abundance for the benefit of mankind, too. 18 is selfless, if not somewhat idealistic, and that is a beautiful combination.

The Meaning of 19

The Number 19 combines the energies of 1 and 9; it is said to represent something similar to what number 10 does--showing us that endings often provide the best and freshest new beginnings. 19 is the number that reveals your divine purpose and connects you with that experience. It's about the inherent stability that can be provided by self-help, and it demonstrates the changes you can incorporate into your life when you are able to face your darkest sides.

The Meaning of 20

The Number 20 combines the energies of 2 and 0; it is said to represent that harmony is coming your way as long as you live with compassion, love, and connection to your intuition. 20 also encourages action with others that validates these gifts of compassion, love, and intuition. Through appropriate action, harmony can be established, and 20 demonstrates that beautiful and liberating potential.

The Meaning of 21

The Number 21 combines the energies of 2 and 1; it is said to represent pure energy in expression, whether verbally, physically, or metaphysically. 21 is a manifestation number as well as a transformative one, and it encourages taking new directions with your new modes of expression. 21 accompanies charisma and genuine communication with others, demonstrating a more evolved version of the self.

The Meaning of 22

The Number 22 combines the energies of 2 and 2; it is said to represent accomplishment and acquired power. 22 is also a number representative of successful partnerships, but this could have pertinence for one's vocational endeavors more so than romantic ones. 22 demonstrates how confidence and hard work pay off and how blessings abound when a harmonious life is achieved.

Tarot & Western Astrology (and more)

Every sign of the zodiac in Western astrology relates with an archetypal energy from the tarot deck. This section will show you how to recognize those relations, since they are admittedly less than obvious. It's not so simple to say that Aries links with the Magician because they're both #1 in their respective areas of study. It's not so simple at all but worry not! I'll guide you through the associations, and it will be accessible enough in no time.

Tarot Looks at Aries...

...and sees the Emperor card from the Major Arcana. Both have energies of determination, commitment, applied authority, motivation, loyalty, and reliability. If you're an Aries conducting a reading for yourself (or if you're reading for someone else who's an Aries), choose the Emperor card to represent yourself (or the Aries querent in question) if the reading asks for a card of this type. Additionally, if the Emperor card arises in an Aries person's spread, it likely represents that person him or herself.

Tarot Looks at Taurus...

...and sees the Hierophant card from the Major Arcana. Both are intense and piercing, they cannot be superficial, and they're deeply involved in truth as a tradition. If you're a Taurus conducting a reading for yourself (or if you're reading for someone else who's a Taurus), choose the Hierophant card to represent yourself (or the Taurus querent in question) if the reading asks for a card of this type. Additionally, if the Hierophant card arises in a Taurus person's spread, it likely represents that person him or herself.

Tarot Looks at Gemini...

...and sees the Lovers card from the Major Arcana. Both are involved with turning points, weighty decisions, careful proceedings, and maintaining personal integrity. If you're a Gemini conducting a reading for yourself (or if you're reading for someone else who's a Gemini), choose the Lovers card to represent yourself (or the Gemini querent in question) if the reading asks for a card of this type.

Additionally, if the Lovers card arises in a Gemini person's spread, it likely represents that person him or herself.

Tarot Looks at Cancer...

...and sees the Chariot card from the Major Arcana. Both are transcendent, steady, security-seeking, partially-protected or -shielded freedom-loving, intuitive, and road-opening. If you're a Cancer conducting a reading for yourself (or if you're reading for someone else who's a Cancer), choose the Chariot card to represent yourself (or the Cancer querent in question) if the reading asks for a card of this type. Additionally, if the Chariot card arises in a Cancer person's spread, it likely represents that person him or herself.

Tarot Looks at Leo...

...and sees the Strength card from the Major Arcana. Both are strong, emotional, mental, courageous, and physical. They both prefer to face their problems with grace rather than avoid them entirely. If you're a Leo conducting a reading for yourself (or if you're reading for someone who's a Leo), choose the Strength card to represent yourself (or the Leo querent in question) if the reading asks for a card of this type. Additionally, if the Strength card arises in a Leo person's spread, it likely represents that person him or herself.

Tarot Looks at Virgo...

...and sees the Hermit card from the Major Arcana. Both are purposeful yet slow, wary yet innocent, experienced and wise yet young at heart, exploratory but only on the inside, and open to the world yet guarded. If you're a Virgo conducting a reading for yourself (or if you're reading for someone who's a Virgo), choose the Hermit card to represent yourself (or the Virgo querent in question) if the reading asks for a card of this type. Additionally, if the Hermit card arises in a Virgo person's spread, it likely represents that person him or herself.

Tarot Looks at Libra...

...and sees the Justice card from the Major Arcana. Both are desirous, emotional, light-hearted, righteous, fair, and justice-oriented. Both also should be careful to note the difference between what is desire versus what is need. If you're a Libra conducting a reading for yourself (or if you're reading for someone else who's a Libra), choose the Justice card to represent yourself (or the Libra querent in question) if the reading asks for a card of this type. Additionally, if the Justice card arises in a Libra person's spread, it likely represents that person him or herself.

Tarot Looks at Scorpio...

...and sees the Death card from the Major Arcana. Both are intense, fascinated by transformation, interested in rebirth, enigmatic, changeable, and introspective. They can both also be extremely personal or utterly detached, for they contain so many extremes. If you're a Scorpio conducting a reading for yourself (or if you're reading for someone else who's a Scorpio), choose the Death card to represent yourself (or the Scorpio querent in question) if the reading asks for a card of this type. Additionally, if the Death card arises in a Scorpio person's spread, it likely represents that person him or herself.

Tarot Looks at Sagittarius...

...and sees the Temperance card from the Major Arcana. Both are gifted mediators and social balancers, understanding leaders, and conscious adventurers. If you're a Sagittarius conducting a reading for yourself (or if you're reading for someone who's a Sagittarius), choose the Temperance card to represent yourself (or the Sagittarius querent in question) if the reading asks for a card of this type.

Additionally, if the Temperance card arises in a Sagittarius person's spread, it likely represents that person him or herself.

Tarot Looks at Capricorn...

...and sees the Devil card from the Major Arcana. Both are shadowy yet skilled, guarded yet knowledgeable, intense yet internally playful, reflective yet confident, and restrictive yet protective of others. If you're a Capricorn conducting a reading for yourself (or if you're reading for someone who's a Capricorn), choose the Devil card to represent yourself (or the Capricorn querent in question) if the reading asks for a card of this type. Additionally, if the Devil card arises in a Capricorn person's spread, it likely represents that person him or herself.

Tarot Looks at Aquarius...

...and sees the Star card from the Major Arcana. Both are enlightened, optimistic, spiritual, leaders, altruistic, and humanitarian. If you're an Aquarius conducting a reading for yourself (or if you're reading for someone else who's an Aquarius), choose the Star card to represent yourself (or the Aquarius querent in question) if the reading asks for a card of this type. Additionally, if the Star card arises in an Aquarius person's spread, it likely represents that person him or herself.

Tarot Looks at Pisces...

...and sees the Moon card from the Major Arcana. Both are dreamy, idealistic, potentially deluded, intuitive, emotional, strong, compassionate, creative, moody, and subtle. If you're a Pisces conducting a reading for yourself (or if you're reading for some else who's a Pisces), choose the Moon card to represent yourself (or the Pisces querent in question) if the reading asks for a card of this type. Additionally, if the Moon card arises in a Pisces person's spread, it likely represents that person him or herself.

Tarot Looks at Water Signs…

…and sees the suit of Cups. Whether your wateriness comes from your Western zodiac sign (Cancer, Scorpio, and Pisces are water signs), your Eastern zodiac sign (Rat and Pig are water signs), your internal Ayurvedic constitution (a.k.a. – your Dosha (Pitta and Kapha constitutions are water-influenced), or otherwise, those associated with the element of water will connect best with the suit of Cups. If Cups arise for you in a reading, they will signify positivity and alignment on your soul mission or life path. If you're looking for a card to demonstrate yourself as a water sign, choose any of the water sign cards (the Chariot, Death, or the Moon), or choose one of the court/face cards in the suit of Cups.

Tarot Looks at Fire Signs…

…and sees the suit of Wands. Whether your fire energy comes from your Western zodiac sign (Aries, Leo, and Sagittarius are fire signs), your Eastern zodiac sign (Snake and Horse are fire signs), your internal Ayurvedic constitution or Dosha (Pitta is primarily fire-influenced), or otherwise, those associated with the element of fire will connect best with the suit of Wands. If Wands arise for you in a reading, they will signify positivity and alignment on your soul mission or life path. If you're looking for a card to demonstrate yourself as a fire sign, choose any of the fire sign cards (the Emperor, Strength, or Temperance), or choose one of the court cards in the suit of wands.

Tarot Looks at Air Signs…

…and sees the suit of Swords. Whether your airiness comes from your Western zodiac sign (Gemini, Libra, and Aquarius are air signs), your internal Ayurvedic constitution or Dosha (Vata is primarily air-influenced), or otherwise (the Eastern zodiac has no alignment with the element of air; they substitute for elements of metal and wood instead), those associated with the element of air will connect best with the suit of Swords. If Swords arise for you in a reading, they will signify positivity and alignment on your soul mission or life path. If you're looking for a card to demonstrate yourself as an air sign, choose any of the air sign cards (the Lovers, Justice, and the Star), or choose one of the court cards in the suit of Swords.

Tarot Looks at Earth Signs...

...and sees the suit of Pentacles. Whether your earthiness comes from your Western zodiac sign (Taurus, Virgo, and Capricorn are earth signs), your Eastern zodiac sign (Dog, Sheep, Ox, and Dragon are earth signs), your internal Ayurvedic constitution or Dosha (Kapha is primarily earth-influenced), or otherwise, those associated with the element of Earth will connect best with the suit of Pentacles. If Pentacles arise for you in a reading, they will signify positivity and alignment on your soul mission or life path. If you're looking for a card to demonstrate yourself as an earth sign, choose any of the earth sign cards (the Hierophant, the Hermit, or the Devil), or choose one of the court cards in the suit of Pentacles.

Chapter 7: Moving Beyond the Deck

If you're like me, this knowledge about the tarot isn't enough. You're already getting your own deck (or collection of decks), you're working with the knowledge, and you're ready to do something with it! If you're like me, you're interested in thinking about how to turn tarot into a career (or at least a "side hustle").

This chapter is dedicated to helping you follow that path, if you wish to do so. Chapter 7 guides you through what vocational tarot is all about, how to get started, what business options exist, and even a 5-step guide for people that relate to this path. If you're drawn to make your living with the assistance of tarot, this chapter is devoted to you.

Using the Tarot Vocationally

Using a metaphysical practice like tarot to start a financial and lifelong vocation is not the easiest task, but it is a pure, righteous, and high-vibration one. Vocational tarot reading can be a remote job, or it can be extremely up-close and personal, depending on what you're comfortable with. You could run an app, or you could run a shop. You could offer private readings, or you could do public work. You could also spread your gifts through word of mouth and see who comes to you.

When you intend to start a business around metaphysics, or tarot specifically, remember that it's best to diversify. If you have the means, open a metaphysical shop–not just a psychic studio. In that shop, however, offer a section for tarot card readings for whomever desires. If you don't have the means, start small and make as many face-to-face connections with people as possible! You never know who will end up wanting to donate based on your gifts.

How to Get Started

The best way to get started with this goal is to define your basics. Consider the following questions:

- Where and with whom are you willing (and not willing) to work?
- What exactly will you offer? Will there be more than just tarot readings? Will you offer specific spreads only?
- Will you insist on qualifications met by clients beforehand?
- What are you offering that's different from others in your area doing the same thing?
- What will your prices be? How will you collect payment? Will you have any sort of sliding scale for payment? If so, for how long–just until you're established or always?
- How will you promote yourself?
- Will you use social media? If so, which sites?
- Can you program, or do you have a programmer buddy? Can you (or that person) make an app to share your work?
- Can you create a website?
- Have you considered Etsy for your platform to start?

- Is there a social media platform you already have that you can expand to take this venture on?
- How do you imagine your business will grow?
- Are you fearful of taking things online or of doing things in person?

Ask yourself all these questions and more, for it's immeasurably helpful to know where your boundaries are from the start and what your basics of business happen to be.

Business Options

- Offer weekly tarot readings in any public space (to start). Options for spaces to host you include cafes, diners, libraries, parks, and more.
- Pair up with local businesses to host tarot nights for Girls' Nights Out and Date Nights.
- Create an app to share your knowledge.
- Create a podcast or YouTube channel to share your knowledge.
- Make your initial business "storefront" a social media page.
- Start a blog about your knowledge to get your energy out there.
- Similarly, write tarot-inspired or -based articles for local magazines and newspapers.
- You can even try to get your own tarot column in your hometown paper to help promote yourself.
- Buy and establish your own literal storefront that you'll have for just psychic and tarot readings (or for metaphysical materials sales, too).
- Create a website with options for virtual tarot readings via email, for example.
- Design your own tarot deck and try to get it "published."
- Write your own tarot book and work to get that published.

- Create a tarot retreat for high-vibration individuals in your town or city.
- Offer Skype or phone-based sessions and leave fliers with your number around town.
- Find a mentor business owner and pair with him or her to promote your wares.
- Similarly, offer weekly tarot readings at your local bookstore or metaphysical shop.

General 5-Step Guide for Tarot Practitioners in Business

For those of you who are ready to follow this path with tarot and take it seriously, the following guide will hopefully provide the logistical or ideological backbone you need to build this tarot empire for yourself (and others).

Step 1 – Start Small

For those just starting off with this transition, it really helps to start small. Especially if you're not the most confident tarot card reader, working one-on-one with others for a while can really give you the boost of energy, certainty, and privacy that you need to begin trusting yourself deeply with these cards. Keep your expectations of your business low so that you can be easily surprised when things start to take off. You're welcome to start planning the infrastructure of your future business, but I recommend not getting *too* caught up in details at this phase of your journey. The first phase is about exploring the options, meeting some people, doing confident readings, and remembering your passion in the first place.

Step 2 – Start Local

A great way to break into the local scene is to start local and work with business owners whose ethics and vibes align with the energies of tarot. Find a local vegetarian or vegan restaurant and get to know the owner, patrons, and employees! You might find your first clients in this base of people. Furthermore, try metaphysical stores, bookstores of all types, coffee shops, and high-vibration shops of all other kinds. Seek out like-minded people, give them a trial reading, and see if they'll promote your work. Make relationships with local business owners, and you might have a Friday or Saturday space to host readings in no time. Connect with other high-vibration healers in your area, too. If you can find them personally, great! If you have to find them virtually, through social media or otherwise, that's fine too. Make connections with these people for you never know who you'll team up with in the future.

Step 3 – Find a Mentor

You never know who might support you, so don't be afraid to reach out to potential patrons for mentorship, too! Local business owners are wonderful, but you could also start socializing with other lovers of divination in order to find yourself a true metaphysical mentor. In fact, this stage of your journey isn't mandatory, but it can help substantially to develop your future business plan. For example, imagine that you've begun hanging out extensively at the local metaphysical store. You chat up the owner every time you come in, and he or she really appreciates your hard work, your passion, and your budding expertise. With a little more talking, you realize that this person is also devoted to tarot (as well as some other things), and you begin taking weekly lessons with him or her. Voilà-- mentor achieved!

Step 4 – Have Pride

One of the most important steps to perfect before you can start up that future business of yours is that you're going to have to maintain immaculate pride and confidence in yourself, your psychic abilities, and your tarot knowledge. Keep a consistent practice until you truly remember all the card meanings; then, take your skills out into the world and wow some people! When people respond positively, use that good energy to boost your self-image and your sense of pride. If people respond negatively, remind yourself that you probably just accosted them with truth! Don't feel too bad, and don't doubt yourself. No matter how people respond, remember your love of tarot, your careful study of it, and your blossoming passion to share it! You're following your purpose, and that insists you follow your path with pride.

Step 5 – Move on Up

Once you've worked through the first 4 steps, it's time to start increasing your scope. You're making connections with local business owners, and you're establishing a clientele. Now's the time to make a social media page for your work so people can start leaving reviews. If you can afford it, promote your page so that anyone interested in metaphysics nearby will find your business without issue. Promote yourself with fliers, by word of mouth, and through posters placed in public spaces that have sign-ups for readings on them. Grow your business bit by bit, and soon enough, you may find yourself with a space to call your office or even your very own shop! Troubleshoot as you go along by asking customers to provide honest reviews of your work, and as long as you're in touch with your higher self, you'll be sure to succeed.

I applaud anyone who aims to turn his or her love of tarot into a vocation. If you relate to this message, I'm proud of you for finding your passion and for being so willing to work with others as your work in the world. I'm also proud of you for embracing your potential as a healer and teacher of others. I know that things may be bumpy for you in the times ahead, but they'll surely settle out in time.

If you encounter hardship, take a step back, and try to remember why you were so drawn to tarot at first. If you ever feel dejected, remember what you loved about tarot and what it gave you when your work started out. Remember these exciting origins to cure any malaise, disinterest, or imbalance.

Promise me that you'll use your abilities for goodness, healing, and growth, and above all else: promise me you'll never lie to someone during their reading because you think you're protecting him or her. Truth and knowledge are light, and to withhold these things from someone is to shed darkness on that light. You're a light-worker if you feel drawn to tarot as a vocation, and now's the time to put that light to work.

Conclusion

Throughout this book, you've encountered information about the history of tarot, each card in the deck, how to choose and then use your deck, and how tarot can change your life. Now, you've completed reading each chapter, and by making it to the end of the book, you deserve a congratulations! Well done, and thank you for making it to the final pages.

Now, it's time to put all this theory into practice. If you haven't been looking at your deck while you were reading–or if you weren't trying out the spreads, memorization tips, and exercises as you went along–now is the time to start trying everything out!

Get your hands on your own beautiful deck of tarot cards, and let yourself experience their beauty, knowledge, and wisdom first-hand. Sit down with your cards spread out around you and take in their mastery before trying out a few spreads for yourself. It's going to be a beautiful adventure for you, and I wish you nothing but the best.

If you've appreciated this book or found it useful for your tarot practice, please feel free to leave a review on Amazon about what you liked! Similarly, if you think my approach could be strengthened or changed in any way, please let me know about that as well.

Thank you again for making it to the end of *Tarot: An Essential Beginner's Guide to Psychic Tarot Reading, Tarot Card Meanings,*

Tarot Spreads, Numerology, and Astrology. I hope you found the experience useful, and I wish you all the best as you journey into tarot for yourself. Good luck!

Check out another book by Kimberly Moon

www.ingramcontent.com/pod-product-compliance
Lightning Source LLC
Chambersburg PA
CBHW030110100526
44591CB00009B/352